Grieg

BRIAN SCHLOTEL

GRIEG

BBC MUSIC GUIDES

ARIEL MUSIC
BBC PUBLICATIONS

To my music students at Kingston Polytechnic, especially those who, over the years, have recorded all Grieg's 142 songs with me.

Published by BBC Publications
A division of BBC Enterprises Ltd
35 Marylebone High Street, London W1M 4AA

First published 1986
© Brian Schlotel 1986

ISBN 0 563 20479 6

Typeset in 10/11 pt Garamond by Phoenix Photosetting, Chatham
Printed in England by Mackays of Chatham Ltd

Contents

Acknowledgements

I would like to thank the members of the Grieg Committee of Oslo University (Chairman: Professor Finn Benestad), and the staff of Bergen Public Library for much help. For English translations of Grieg's letters I am indebted to David Monrad-Johansen's *Edvard Grieg* (New York, 1945), and to Bjarne Kortsen's *Grieg the Writer*, Volumes 1 and 2 (Bergen 1972). The English titles to Grieg's music I have usually used are those of the catalogue of works in John Horton's *Grieg* (London, 1974) which are accurately translated from the original Norwegian. I am also indebted to these recent publications by Norwegian scholars:

Dag Schjelderup-Ebbe, *Edvard Grieg* 1852–1867 (Oslo, 1964)

Bjarne Kortsen: Grieg's String Quartet and Robert Heckman (*Music and Letters* January, 1968)

Bjarne Kortsen: Four Unknown Cantatas by Grieg (Bergen, 1972)

Introduction

Currently a process of re-discovering Grieg is going on. This is being given a boost by the magnificent new Complete Edition of his music in twenty volumes, edited and annotated by the Grieg Committee of Oslo University, and published since 1977 by Peters at the rate of one or two volumes each year.

Far more of his music is now available on disc than ever before, including the recording of the complete piano music by the enterprising Stockholm company of Bis; and whereas listeners usually had to be content with the short suites from *Peer Gynt* and *Sigurd Jorsalfar*, recordings of the complete incidental music for these plays are now available. A Norwegian choir and soloists visited London in 1978 to give concert performances of the unfinished opera *Olav Trygvason* and the cantata *Landsighting*, and these performances were issued on records. Even rarer works like *The Mountain Thrall* for baritone and orchestra, and the *Four Psalms* for unaccompanied choir, have had BBC broadcasts in the 1980s.

In late Victorian and Edwardian times Grieg's music became extremely popular. His piano pieces in particular – often well within the technical grasp of the amateur – were to be found in most musical homes, not only in Britain, but throughout Europe and North America. In the neo-classical 1920s a reaction set in, and it became fashionable to show indifference to Grieg's music for the next half century, and to dismiss it in the phrase coined by Debussy as 'a pink bon-bon stuffed with snow'.

Some of Grieg's music always remained in the repertoire, however, and ensured that he continued to be known to concert-goers, radio listeners and discophiles. But his fame rested on a very few works – such as the Piano Concerto, the *Peer Gynt Suites*, the song *I love thee*. Now that performers, promoters and gramophone companies are becoming more adventurous, the present book aims to be a guide to virtually *all* Grieg's music, and, in aiding music-lovers on their path of re-discovering Grieg, it promises rich rewards among the seventy-four published works of a wonderfully original tone-poet.

Grieg was the first significant composer to make the world of nature central to his musical thought. And it was primarily the scenery of Norway that inspired him, more especially that round Bergen, where he was born on 15 June 1843, spent his boyhood, and much of his adult life. Bergen lies in an environment well suited to the nourishing of his imagination: to the north and south are the long Sogne and Hardanger fiords, to the west the North Atlantic's bracing winds roll foaming waves landwards, past countless islands, crags and skerries, while to the east rise the hills with their pinewoods and vast views – the district which the Norwegians themselves call the Westland. Grieg acknowledged this influence and expanded upon it when he wrote to his American biographer Finck: 'The traditional way of life of the Norwegian people, together with Norway's legends, Norway's history, Norway's natural scenery, stamped itself on my creative imagination from my earliest years.'

To give expression to this wonder-world of Norwegian inspiration Grieg created a musical style completely original to himself. Various influences can, of course, be detected, both from art-music and from folk-music, and during his student years he was absorbing academic ideas that were going to be useful for his musical language. His individuality thrived, however, because he was able to assimilate these various elements, and a strong *personal* voice speaks out in nearly all his compositions from the age of twenty-two. For instance, take the three-note phrase that we could call the 'Grieg Motif':

Ex.1

major form   minor (or modal) form

This melodic line can be found in the music of many composers, including Bach, also in the folk-music of many lands. But Grieg used it much more than any previous composer and he integrates it into his own melodic style.

Again, amongst the characteristics of Norwegian folk-music, five can be singled out thus:

1   Many melodies making the dominant of the scale their focal point.
2   Fondness for modal scales.
3   Inclusion of many unstable scales which fluctuate between major, minor and modes.
4   Frequent changes of tonality during melodies.
5   Characteristic uses of ornaments like the upper mordent.

Scandinavian composers of the 1860s, such as the Danes Horneman and Hartmann, used many of these traits when they wanted to cultivate northern colour. Grieg, who had studied with Gade, may have been stimulated by their example, but he made far, far more inspired use of the idioms – firstly because he uses them much more imaginatively, and secondly because with him they become part of the expression of a forceful creative language. He had had a thorough grounding in academic techniques during his four years at the Leipzig Conservatoire, and this gave him the freedom to absorb other ideas and place them on a firm foundation. For instance, he was able to take modal melodies and harmonise them using the most advanced chromatic techniques of his own day, which again resulted in an entirely Griegian type of blend.

Grieg's sources of inspiration and his original style enabled him to become, just as he wished, a truly Norwegian composer. However, his status as an international composer was achieved because he was able to make this national art into a truly cosmopolitan one that reached out across cultures and continents, and by the time he was fifty he was one of the most widely known and performed composers in the world.

Piano Works

In one of his letters Grieg speaks of his admiration for 'the incredibly terse vigour of expression, the peculiar flair for getting so much said in so few words' that is found in the *Edda* – that wonderful collection of heroic and mythological verses composed by Norwegians, or men of Norwegian descent, in Iceland between the ninth and twelfth centuries. 'The deeper the heart's distress, the more contained and cryptic the wording,' wrote Grieg.

In the best of his work that is exactly what he himself achieves. Few composers can equal him in the *brevity* with which he is able to set a mood or describe an experience. It is interesting to see that this gift, or the embryo of it, was there from the very first. The Bergen Public Library, to which Grieg bequeathed all the manuscripts still in his possession, has a collection of 24 *Small Pieces for Piano*, his earliest surviving compositions, written when he was about fifteen. These show that his aptitude for the small-scale statement was already present: the pieces tend to be only about thirty to fifty bars long, and the shortest is only thirteen bars.

It was pieces such as these that Grieg would have played to the famous nineteenth-century Norwegian violinist Ole Bull when they met in the summer of 1858. Bull was convinced that here were the seeds of rare musical talent and persuaded Grieg's parents to send the boy to the Leipzig Conservatoire, where he would have the benefit of the most thorough and prestigious musical training then available anywhere in the world.

In later life Grieg constantly voiced his dissatisfaction with the Leipzig Conservatoire, probably because it failed to help him find himself, but his exercise books, preserved in the Bergen Public Library, show him working steadily through all the studies in harmony, counterpoint and fugue usual for a theoretical musical training during his four years there. The first published result was his Op. 1, *Four Pieces for Piano*, which he performed himself at a Leipzig concert in March 1862 when he was awarded his diploma. The first piece shows that he had learnt much from Schumann's piano style in his use of figurations, and of inner contrapuntal voices, and in fact all the pieces speak the language of German romanticism. The second is the most interesting and prophetic of things to come, with its simple diatonic melody, harmonised in a way that draws on the ultimate chromatic techniques of the day.

Composing piano pieces occupied Grieg throughout the whole of his career, from these early student days to his most novel, pioneering works of the early twentieth century. The majority of these are short works, in which he could display his skill as a miniaturist. All of them are 'pianistic' in their layout too, because the piano was Grieg's instrument. It was his second study at the Conservatoire and throughout his life he appeared on the concert stage to play his own works. Thus the melodies and harmonies are always effective in the register in which they appear, all passage work lies well under the fingers, the possibilities of the instrument are constantly drawn on to produce 'pianistic' effects, and Grieg always seems able to fulfil the precise nature of his keyboard aims, whether it is cultivating a mood in an easy Lyric Piece, or producing a virtuoso work like the *Ballade*, Op. 24.

After he had completed his studies at Leipzig, Grieg, now nineteen, settled in Denmark, hoping to break away in his music from German influences. He enjoyed being in a circle of Danish writers and musicians, and in the compositions of this 'Danish period' we find a new lightness and grace in his works. This sunnier outlook is shown in his next piano pieces, *Six Poetic Tone Pictures*, Op. 3, composed in 1863, and published in Copenhagen in the following year. Then quite suddenly the next group of piano pieces, *Humoreskes*, Op. 6, show he had taken a tremendous step forward in 'finding himself' and his Norwegian self too. The cause is to be attributed to the influence of his compatriot, the young composer Rikard Nordraak (1842–66). Nordraak seems to have had a tremendously striking and charismatic personality, and he had an immense interest in his Norwegian and Viking roots. Musical studies in Berlin, where he clashed violently with his German teachers, convinced him that the future of Norwegian music was not through German rules and forms, but through the dances and songs of Norwegian folk-music.

When the two men had first met in Copenhagen's Tivoli Gardens in the summer of 1863, Nordraak had been rather reserved about Grieg, criticising him for his one-sided views and his exclusive predilection for Schumann, as is shown by a letter of Nordraak to his Danish friend Louis Halbeck written on 24 May 1864. However, Grieg, in later life, when asked about Nordraak, only remembered his charismatic side, and was probably recalling events that occurred during and after February 1865 when both were settled in Copenhagen and had formed a firm friendship, joining together in forming 'Euterpe', a society for promotng northern music.

Writing to Aimar Gronwald in 1881, Grieg said:

When you ask about Nordraak's influence on me, it is as you suppose, that his view of our folk-music strengthened my own. But my national enthusiasm had already awakened before I knew him, though it had not borne fruit in my art. It was the impact of our meeting that caused the productive outburst of this enthusiasm . . . We were completely unalike in spite of our mutual sympathy. And just because of this, we could influence each other fruitfully.

Also, Grieg wrote to Iver Holter on 9 February 1897:

Nordraak's importance for me is *not* exaggerated. It is like this: through him, and through him alone, light came to me . . . I was longing to find expression for the best that was in me – a best that lay a thousand miles from Leipzig and its atmosphere; but that it lay in love of my fatherland and in my feeling for the great, melancholy Westland nature I did not know and would never perhaps have found out if I had not, through Nordraak, been led to self-examination. This had its first result in the *Humoreskes*, Op. 6, dedicated to Nordraak, in which the direction of development is plainly shown.

We can readily agree that in the *Humoreskes* Grieg, for the first time, found a style entirely his own. On to his chromatic harmonies are grafted ideas suggested by Norwegian folk-music: drones, bare fifths, parallel fifths, ornaments, and tiny motifs repeated, varied and joined together to form long sections; while the rhythms of traditional dances are found, with the first and fourth *Humoreskes* related to the *Springing Dance*, and the third to the *Halling*. His handling of the keyboard is entirely original too, with the writing for two or three voices in widely spaced registers (Ex. 2), and the percussive effects (Ex. 3).

Ex.2   Humoreske no.1: Tempo di Valse

Ex.3 Humoreske no.4: Allegro all Burla – più Allegro

Nordraak was delighted with his friend's pieces. When Grieg played him the very *rustic* Minuet that is no. 3, he broke in: 'Yes, that is as if I had written it myself.' The strange thing is, though, that Nordraak's music is not at all chromatic, and much of it is badly lacking in technique; he achieved nothing like the *Humoreskes*. It was obviously not his music but his *personality* and his *ideas* that influenced Grieg.

The next month, June 1865, while Grieg was living at the home of a talented amateur musician, Benjamin Feddersen, at Rungsted near Copenhagen, came the Piano Sonata in E minor, Op. 7 – destined to be the longest of Grieg's works for solo piano, though even then it modestly runs for only about twenty-three minutes' playing time.

'Whether it was the enchanting surroundings or the stimulating air that inspired me, I cannot say,' wrote Grieg. 'Enough that in eleven days I had composed my piano sonata and very soon after my first violin sonata.' A fuller discussion of Grieg's use of sonata-form will be given in the chapter on his chamber music. Here it is best to take the Piano Sonata on its own terms, an exuberant work, written in the full flush of youthful inspiration and enthusiasm.

The Sonata is notable for its great melodiousness, while an air of novelty arises from the melodic lines leading at times into modal forms, for example in the second movement: Mixolydian in bars 9–13, Dorian in bar 18. The themes, too, are enriched by typically Griegian harmony as when the second subject in the first movement is recapitulated over an extended dominant pedal. Fresh effects abound in the harmony, as here in the slow movement (Ex. 4), when Grieg uses one of his favourite devices of resolving discords in unusual ways:

Ex.4

Andante molto

The first movement opens with the bold theme of the first subject making its impetuous, headlong rush down the keyboard, and a well-contrasted second subject follows in G major. The development explores various possibilities of the first theme through many keys, never losing its momentum, until the headlong rush of the recapitulation begins. The lyrical second movement is in the best tradition of Scandinavian composers, who so often make their slow movements rival their famed sweet liqueurs. Grieg's ultra-sweetness is provided with a short *poco più vivo* middle section, an apt foil before the augmented return of the first section. The *Alla Menuetto* third movement inhabits much the same world as the second *Humoreske* and is an early example of Grieg's predilection for using old-fashioned forms as a disguise. It is only a thin disguise, however, for melody and harmony are Griegian, especially the exquisitely realised middle section. The finale is particularly notable for the poetic second subject, and the way that this is expanded in the recapitulation into a glorious paean, which brings the work to an end in a mood of youthful confidence in the future. The work was issued by Breitkopf and Härtel, the leading German publishers, in 1865. When Grieg brought out a new edition with Peters in 1887 he cut bars 31 to 55 of the original finale. This seems rather pointless self-criticism, and the fuller version is to be preferred.

The next piano work was also influenced by Nordraak, but in tragic circumstances. Grieg had been spending the winter in Rome having a busy round of artistic and social engagements with Scandinavian friends living there, when on 6 April 1866 news reached him that, in lonely and impoverished circumstances and after months of illness, Nordraak had died of consumption in Berlin on 20 March. Grieg's diary records:

> Letter from Feddersen! [a large black cross is drawn]. The saddest news that I could receive – Nordraak is dead! – he, my only friend, my only great hope for Norwegian art! Oh, how dark it has suddenly become around me! And I have no human being here who can rightly understand my grief, let me then take refuge in music, it never fails at the hour of sorrow! . . . Composed a funeral march for Nordraak.

The march conveys a mood of terrible grief and anguish (Ex. 5).

Ex.5

With perhaps in the A major Trio section (composed the following day) a glimpse of hopes never to be realised.

THE LYRIC PIECES

From 1866 Grieg settled in the Norwegian capital, which was known as Christiania from 1624 to 1925 (when it was re-named Oslo), and joined the long procession of composers from Mozart to César Franck who, in order to make ends meet, have trudged round their home cities giving piano lessons. The fees he received as a young man from German and Danish publishers were derisorily small, and royalty arrangements usually nil. Not until 1883 was Grieg able to get a secure income from his compositions, when the Leipzig firm of Peters (which had previously rejected many of his best works) offered him an exclusive contract, after seeing his popularity with the musical public fast accelerating.

Undoubtedly some of the items in the first book of Lyric Pieces, Op. 12, originated as material for his pupils. But then so did fine works by Scarlatti and Haydn. The Lyric Pieces make ideal teaching material for all grades, yet they are so much more. The first book became a best seller throughout Europe – it was just what was wanted: modern music that was extremely attractive, and yet not technically demanding. It is interesting to note that when the forty-year-old Grieg made his agreement with Peters, one of the first things they asked for was a new set of Lyric Pieces. These too became best sellers, as did books three to ten, which were published at intervals between 1886 and 1901.

The sixty-six Lyric Pieces are like a huge gallery of water-colours in which delicate hues predominate. Here we have above all impressions of nature, drawn by a sincere artist who identifies in all sympathy with his subjects. There are also impressions of stories, dances and moods. Almost all have the imprint of Grieg's original genius and the collection wonderfully exemplifies his gift for small-scale mastery.

Book I starts off with a charmingly Schumannesque *Arietta*, in which the second half subtly varies the first half's melody and harmony to make a most satisfying growth of the idea. The *Waltz* in A minor which follows again shows subtle development when the left-hand melody of the A major middle section is used to make a coda in which the melody is transferred to the treble, but the wavering of the piece between major and minor continues to the very end – one of Grieg's most characteristic traits. *The Watchman's Song* represents a story, for in the middle section, headed 'Ghosts of the Night', he blows his horn at the apparitions four times until they finally disappear, leaving him to resume his lantern-lit patrol. Here too, by shortening the recapitulation and making it veer momentarily into the relative minor, Grieg provides a pleasing development for the whole.

It is a pity Grieg did not make more use of the kind of development which has been noted in the first three Lyric Pieces. The remaining five pieces in Book I, and the vast majority of those that were to follow, rely to an unfortunate extent on repetition. This is one of the weaknesses of Grieg, particularly late Grieg. Sometimes he is defended because the loneliness of his artistic position in Norway meant that he had no good colleagues to hand who could advise him in conversation, or stimulate him by their example.

In Book II, Op. 38, the exhilarating little *Waltz* started life as a Christmas present for his fiancée's sister in 1866, and it shows the possibility that others of the Lyric Pieces were composed well before the date of their publication. The exquisite *Melody* has often suffered in performance from having the time signature misprinted as C in the popular German edition, whereas it should be ₵; this is given correctly in the new Oslo edition.

Book III, Op. 43, published in 1886, is one of the two outstanding sets (the other being Book V). The brightly gleaming *Butterfly* and the sprightly *Little Bird* are masterpieces of miniature programme music, while the *Lonely Wanderer* and *Love Song* evoke powerful moods – the one of home-sickness and weariness, the other of rapture. The third piece of the set illustrates the fact that Grieg was not among those composers who invent their titles *after* their pieces are composed, or anyhow say they do. Among the letters to his friend Frants Beyer is one dated Copenhagen, 26 April 1886:

What do you say to a quiet morning in the boat or out between skerries and cliffs? The other day I was so full of this longing that it took shape as a quiet little song of thanksgiving . . . If Troldhaugen's surroundings had been grander, the tone would have been different, but I am happy with them as they are and out of this quiet happiness . . . a piece of music was born.

And Grieg enclosed a manuscript of *In my Native Land*.

The sixth piece is the well-known *To the Spring*. This paints vividly all that the warmth and brightness of spring mean to the northern mind, after the bitter winter with its long hours of darkness. In the music are portrayed the slow beginnings of spring, when the first pale flowers appear, and the streams start to trickle again. Then the tremendous power of melting snows unleashes the majesty of the rushing waterfalls. Finally the opening melody reappears in an extended form, enriched with flowing arpeggios, full of happiness, sunshine and hope.

Book IV, Op. 47, published in 1888, has two notable themes in *Valse-Impromptu* and *Melody* which exploit the minor scale in an exotic Griegian way, and also particularly characteristic and attractive examples of the Norwegian dance-forms *Springing Dance* and *Halling*. The latter is an exact transcription for piano of the one Grieg had composed for his *Peer Gynt* music (Ex. 6). Its rasping drone bass, imitating the Hardanger fiddle's sympathetic strings, continues through the whole thirty-eight bars of the piece, creating wild, free harmonies, and giving the feeling of the deep, remote Norwegian countryside (as, of course, is its purpose in *Peer Gynt*):

Ex.6

Book V, Op. 54, composed in 1891, is perhaps the most wonderful of all the ten books. The six pieces are outstanding examples of Grieg's art, and four of them have become widely known to concert audiences as the composer orchestrated them into his *Lyric Suite* (discussed below on pages 88–9).

The set starts with a portrait of a dreamy *Shepherd Boy*, tending his herd high up in the Norwegian mountains, far from all human contact. The freedom of the vast spaces is expressed in the constantly changing, irregular rhythms; the depth of the introspection by the finely etched chromaticism. In the *Gangar* (or *Processional Dance*) the crisp effect of sunshine on sparkling snow is irresistibly recreated by the chain of sevenths, while distant views are cultivated in the highest register of the keyboard. All the magic of a warm summer night is captured in *Notturno*, while the lively *Scherzo* has a middle section of the utmost melodic charm. The *Trolls' March* has an effective first section as these little men of Norwegian folklore come nearer and nearer, and the middle section reveals a beautiful green vale after they have passed. But the piece suffers from Grieg's unfortunate over-dependence on ternary form when the first part is merely repeated, whereas a more imaginative design would have been thought out by so many other composers who handled similar 'processional' ideas – Borodin, Wagner, Debussy.

The last piece, *Bell-Ringing*, gains in musical interest precisely because it avoids any formal scheme, and is presented as a constantly developing tone-picture. By means of bare fifths imitating the harmonies of bells deep in a stark and lonely countryside, the composer gives an extraordinarily vivid piece of impressionism. This evocative scheme, composed many years before Debussy's various piano pieces redolent of bell-ringing, shows Grieg at his most original. The fifths remain the sole texture until almost the very end, when briefly and remotely the chords of organ-playing can be imagined, borne across the still air.

Book VI, Op. 57, composed in 1893, has its tone set by the first piece, the nostalgic *Vanished Days*, and four of its six items are predominantly melancholy, like the last, *Home-sickness*, which doubtless reflects the composer's feelings during the long European concert tours embarked on in his later years. However, the piece is relieved by a bright reminiscence of the Norwegian countryside using a favourite device of Grieg at this time, the major scale with the sharpened fourth. Among the happier pieces is one of memory for the Danish composer Niels W. Gade (1817–90), making one of Grieg's rare uses of canon, and perhaps remembering his composition studies with Gade thirty years before.

Book VII, Op. 62, composed in 1895, includes *Gratitude*, melodious and emotional; the charming *French Serenade*, with its accompaniment imitating a strummed guitar; a picture of one of the tiny, crystal-clear brooklets that tumble down Norwegian hillsides, bubbling over countless brown and grey stones; and *Homeward*, conjuring up all the joy and excitement felt by the northern traveller as he journeys towards his well-loved home. The pensive middle section, with its deeper thoughts, provides an admirable foil.

Book VIII, Op. 65, composed in 1896, has the celebrated *Wedding Day at Troldhaugen*, composed for one of Edvard and Nina's wedding anniversaries ('Troldhaugen' being the name of their country house near Bergen). This is the longest Lyric Piece, lasting five or six minutes and making a magnificent concert item with many pianistic devices that exploit the keyboard. The unforgettable melodies are constantly accompanied by bell-ringing effects, especially so in the coda, which conjures up a haze of distant bells, before the final *fffz* chord. Other attractive items are *In Ballad Style* with its stark northern mood, perhaps evoking some dark tale from the Norse sagas; *Peasants' Song* in which any monotony there might have been in repetition of the melody is obviated by the constantly enriched harmonies; and *From Days of Youth* – a rethinking of Op. 57, no. 1, again with the middle section in the major key with the sharpened fourth.

Book IX, Op. 68, published in 1898, contains two especially fine pieces, of which Grieg published orchestrated versions in the same year: *Lullaby*, probably full of tender memories of Grieg's only child, a daughter, who died when only one year old, and scored exquisitely for strings, and *Evening in the Mountains*. The first half of this latter piece has a melody of thirty-eight bars completely unaccompanied – imitating a shepherd boy's pipe, far away among the lonely hills. In the second half the melody is richly harmonised. The orchestral arrangement is for one oboe, one horn and strings. When conducting the work, Grieg used to conceal the oboist, who is given the long solo melody, immediately in front of the conductor's rostrum, so that his sounds seem to be coming from far away and beyond the audience's sight.

The tenth and final book, Op. 71, appeared in 1901. *Once Upon a Time* is virtually the only Lyric Piece using traditional tunes. Here a Swedish and a Norwegian tune are contrasted. *Summer Evening* is one of Grieg's best nature pictures, full of a quiet, rapt intensity. It is followed by *Puck*, a brilliant little *tour de force*. *Quiet of the Woods* is a gentle meditation lit by soft green light filtering through the trees, and full of harmonic ideas that make completely original effects. The *Halling* is the grandest and most technically demanding example of this dance in the Lyric Pieces, and contains the one and only *glissando* in Grieg's compositions – used to great effect to usher in a restatement of the theme in the highest part of the keyboard. *Past and Over*, also headed 'In Memoriam', is a heart-felt poem, whose extreme chromaticism searches us through and through with its searing grief. The Lyric Pieces come to an end with *Recollection*. Here Grieg takes the melody of the first Lyric Piece, Op. 12, no. 1 (Ex. 7(a)), and makes a Lisztian transformation of it, turning it into a kind of *Valse Triste* of bitter-sweet memories (Ex. 7(b)).

Ex.7

Poco Andante e sostenuto   Op.12 no.1

With *Recollection* Grieg, now aged fifty-eight, had decided to bring the series to an end, and was thinking of the twenty-four-year-old piano teacher, just married and at the start of his career, and of all that had happened since. He had achieved riches and world fame, but he had failed to conquer the great forms, as he had wished; he had had a happy marriage, but had lost his only child. These and many other memories would have been going through Grieg's mind, and for anyone who knows the story of his life, the piece is most moving.

Any recital of Lyric Pieces which begins with the *Arietta* and ends with *Recollection* is put at once into an effective framework, with the pianist's individual choice from this wonderful anthology making up the middle. The melodic similarities between the first and the last piece are so strong that the ear of even the inexperienced listener realises the chain of melodies has turned full circle.

The suite *Scenes from Folk Life*, Op. 19, published in 1872, is notable for its middle movement, *The Wedding Procession passes by* – one of the brightest jewels of Grieg's piano music. The charmingly ornamented rustic tunes, and the pianistic idioms, all contribute to its success, but even more so the convincing use of form. The ternary form which we criticised Grieg for using in his *Trolls' March* is here discarded. The procession takes quite a while reaching us, at times obscured by the pinewoods or seeming to make a detour, but finally passes with its extensive line of loud and good-natured humour, while to depict the procession retreating into the distance the composer handles fragments of the main tunes in quite a new way. Grieg regularly included this piece in his recitals. Edouard Lalo borrowed the opening melody of the first movement of the work, *Mountain Tune*, for his *Rapsodie Norvégienne* of 1881, thinking, erroneously, that it was folk-music, and this was a source of grim humour for Grieg. The suite, whose outer movements are more technically demanding than is usual in Grieg, makes some attempt at unity when the main theme of the second movement briefly appears in the last movement, *From the Carnival*.

One of Grieg's solo piano works which makes a fairly regular appearance on the concert platform is his *Ballade* in G minor, Op. 24, composed in 1875. It lasts some nineteen minutes, and consists of a theme and fourteen variations, which exploit many keyboard possibilities, and give the executant considerable chances for displaying his virtuosity. In the words of the traditional air that Grieg uses, the ballad-singer says that there are many songs saying how fine the South is, but he is going to make a song to extol the beauties of the North. The poetic idea would have been attractive to Grieg, who, in the tone-pictures that follow, concentrates almost entirely on the darker aspects of the North, so that we may feel the lure of bleak mountains, sombre pine forests, vast expanses of clear water and bracing winds.

The four *Album Leaves*, Op. 28, make a pleasing set, but in fact were composed at widely different dates. The first of 1864 is written in Grieg's sunny early Danish style; the second of 1874 is extremely chromatic, the third melodious, while the fourth has an attractive story behind its composition. In the spring of 1878, Grieg was sitting in his little work hut – 'just big enough for a composer, a stove and a piano' – by the fiord at Lofthus, feeling melancholy, when he observed from the window rowing boats taking local people to church, and Hardanger fiddlers playing in the bows. He captured the picture in the *Album Leaf*. We hear the composer in dark, pensive mood in the first two pages. Then the villagers' boats glide across the scene and the mood changes completely. They pass, leaving the solitary composer to his musings again, and this time the ternary form is entirely appropriate to the story.

Grieg's next piano work shows him trying to transplant the manner of Liszt's *Hungarian Rhapsodies* to the North, for the *Improvisations on two Norwegian folk-songs*, Op. 29, cultivate an unusually theatrical style for Grieg – though they are effective platform pieces.

In 1884 the citizens of Bergen celebrated the bicentenary of the birth

of Ludwig Holberg, the founder of modern Danish-Norwegian literature. Holberg had spent his orphaned boyhood in Bergen, before going
to the University of Copenhagen. After many travels he settled in
Copenhagen, writing prodigiously, in Danish, books on history, poli-
tics, science and philosophy. In 1721 he became director of the city's
theatre. Until that time no plays had been acted in Denmark except in
German and French. Holberg set out to remedy this, and wrote over a
dozen plays in Danish, most of which were promptly produced. His gift
for satire soon earned him the nick-name, 'Molière of the North'.

Grieg produced two works for the Holberg festivities, the first a
choral cantata, whose première he conducted in light drizzle with a
250-strong male-voice choir in Bergen market place on 3 December,
the actual birth date, and the second the suite for piano, *From Holberg's
Time*, Op. 40. This was premièred on 7 December by the composer
himself in a concert, indoors this time, which also featured another
performance of the cantata. Early in 1885 Grieg scored the suite for
strings, and in sending both versions to his publisher, maintained that
the score for string orchestra was the original. He knew how difficult it
was to get an orchestral work printed, and had it been offered as just an
arrangement, there might have been no hope. However, we may be sure
the publishers did not suspect the subterfuge. The music is thought out
most idiomatically for both forces, for instance the opening (Ex. 8) is
scored thus for the strings (Ex. 9):

Ex.8

Ex.9

We have seen in other works of Grieg how he enjoyed cultivating an old-fashioned touch. He pushes the process furthest in this work, saying he was thinking of the style of the French clavecinistes, who were flourishing at the time of Holberg. Apart from imitating their ornamental flourishes, Grieg uses a number of the characteristic dance rhythms which they favoured, like the Sarabande, and the Rigaudon (a leaping, kicking dance in vogue at the court of Louis XIV). In the third movement too, a favourite formal device of François Couperin is used when a Gavotte is contrasted with a rural-style Musette section, over a drone bass. But the work remains pure Grieg, and it is impossible to imagine any previous composer writing it.

Grieg published his last collection of piano pieces in 1905, called *Moods*. The first piece is a perfect miniature expression in the resigned feeling that came to him more and more in later life. *Night Ride* is a blurred impressionistic painting, with a moonlit rendezvous for its centre-piece. *Students' Serenade* includes a melodious imitation of a male-voice choir. The two gems of the set are *Folk Tune from Valders*, a long pastoral melody in one of the composer's most pleasing and imaginative harmonisations; and *Mountaineer's Song*, remarkable for its echo-effects which give the impression of vast lonely spaces, and which, when treated in strict canon, give strange, bleak harmonies suitable for the snowy, deserted slopes.

Grieg also produced a number of works for two pianos and for piano duet. His parts for second piano to accompany keyboard sonatas by Mozart are not in accordance with modern taste; certainly they are works we should only turn to if we want to hear Grieg rather than Mozart. The Grieg enthusiast may enjoy them on occasions, studying the silver settings that he provides for Mozart's pearls.

An original work for two pianos is the *Old Norwegian Melody with Variations* of 1891. It is an enjoyable piece for two to play, but the quality of inspiration burns nothing like so brightly as it had in the variations of the *Ballade*, Op. 24. The beautiful theme of this duo is *Sigurd and the Troll Bride*, which Grieg had already harmonised in his *Six Norwegian Mountain Tunes for Piano*. Yet it is so strongly characterised by its alternation of major and minor mediants that some monotony in the variations is almost inevitable.

Grieg's many arrangements of his orchestral works for piano duet helped people to get to know them in the pre-gramophone age. But works of this type, like the *Symphonic Dances*, will be considered in the original orchestral form. Pre-eminent among the original works for piano duet are the *Norwegian Dances*, Op. 35. Each of the four dances is built on traditional tunes, imaginatively harmonised and imaginatively laid out for the two players.

Piano Works based on Norwegian folk-music

The four sets of piano music that Grieg published in this category show his strong development as a composer. First came the *25 Norwegian Folk-songs and Dances*, Op. 17, written in 1870, soon after Grieg had discovered the *Old and New Mountain Melodies*, collected and first published in 1853 by the organist and composer Ludwig Lindeman. Lindeman provided a simple accompaniment for these traditional tunes, but Grieg's arrangements are richer, often introduced by a few bars to set the mood, plus a short postlude. Although Grieg generally uses just one statement of the song-themes, the dance-tunes are often repeated three or four times, with a fuller harmonic accompaniment each time.

Next, published in 1875 by Hansen of Copenhagen, without opus number, came the *Six Norwegian Mountain Tunes*, technically undemanding for the pianist, but fresher in the harmonic approach.

The *19 Previously Unprinted Norwegian Folk-songs*, Op. 66, published in 1896, are mostly harmonisations of melodies collected by Grieg's friend Frants Beyer, and show a great step forward in freedom of treatment. Sometimes two or more songs are joined together to make a piece, the pianistic idiom is much freer, the harmonies are quintessentially Griegian, and in the songs he often presents three verses, each treated in a completely different way. For instance in no. 14, *In Ola Valley, in Ola Lake* (the melody which Delius borrowed for his *On Hearing the First Cuckoo in Spring* of 1912), the first statement of this theme is accompanied by gently syncopated bare fourths and fifths; in the second, the melody is transferred to a tenor line played by the left hand, with rich harmonies below and a syncopated drowsy accompaniment above; finally it appears in the treble again and with richly harmonised chromaticisms, which show that Delius was influenced by Grieg's harmonies as well (see Ex. 10 overleaf).

A similar scheme is employed for the three verses of no. 18, *I wander deep in Thought*, a song whose devotional intensity is greatly heightened by Grieg, especially in his seven-bar postlude. The last song, *Gjendine's Lullaby*, is the only folk-melody actually *collected* by Grieg, Gjendine being a herd-girl high up in the Norwegian mountains whom Grieg and Beyer heard on one of their walking holidays. (Her goat-horn also suggested the melody for *Home-sickness* from the sixth book of Lyric

Ex.10

Pieces.) The *Lullaby* is given dark, mountain colouring by the long tonic pedal note which accompanies its first eight, and last three, bars.

With the *Norwegian Peasant Dance-Tunes*, Op. 72, we find Grieg moving firmly into the twentieth century, foreshadowing the music of Bartók in his daring adaptation of folk scales to make new harmonies, and his percussive, abrasive style of piano writing. In his settings of these seventeen *Slåtter* (to give them their correct Norwegian name) Grieg's realisations of Norwegian folk-music reached a new peak. Their genesis makes an interesting story.

The most famous Norwegian folk fiddler of the nineteenth century had been Torgeir Augundsson, who played under the professional name of 'The Miller Boy'. Ole Bull had arranged for him to visit Bergen in 1850 to give some recitals. Now in 1901, just after Grieg had completed the tenth book of Lyric Pieces, he received a letter from Knut Dale, who said he was the last surviving pupil of the Miller Boy, and could anything be done to save his store of tunes, for when he was dead they would be gone forever. Grieg, no violinist himself, sent Knut Dale money to travel to the Norwegian capital, and arranged for him to be met there by the violinist and composer Johan Halvorsen (1864–1935) who would transcribe his tunes. Halvorsen wrote to Grieg on 17 November:

Knut Dale has come. Today we rescued two tunes from oblivion. It is

28

not easy to write them down. There are small turns and trills in them like a trout in a rapid – when you try to get hold of them they are off . . . he had some rhythmic turns, a blending of 2/4 and 6/8 time that made me laugh aloud with delight.

On 3 December Halvorsen posted to Grieg the seventeen *Slåtter* he had notated, commenting on the strange fact that nearly all the D major tunes had a G sharp early on. In sending thanks on 6 December, Grieg said he had been chuckling inwardly with delight as he read the *Slåtter*. He also added that he had discovered folk-songs in the scale of D major with the sharpened fourth as long ago as 1871; it had 'sent the blood rushing to his head', and he had used it in his *Scenes from Folk Life*.

Grieg set to work to make piano pieces from the *Slåtter* the following August. They caused him much trouble, but were finished and despatched to his publishers in February 1903, Grieg insisting that they also printed Halvorsen's violin transcription. Grieg contributed a preface in which he first extolled the raw material from which he worked:

Those who can appreciate such music, will be delighted at the originality, the blending of fine, soft gracefulness with sturdy, almost uncouth power and untamed wildness as regards melody and more particularly rhythm, contained in them. This music – which is handed down to us from an age when the culture of the Norwegian peasant was isolated in its solitary mountain-valleys from the outer world, to which fact it owes its whole originality – bears the stamp of an imagination as daring in its flight as it is peculiar.

He next explained his methods:

My object in arranging the music for the piano was to raise these works of the people to an artistic level, by giving them what I might call a style of musical concord, or bringing them under a system of harmony. Naturally, many of the little embellishments, characteristic of the peasant's fiddle and of their peculiar manner of bowing, cannot be reproduced on the piano, and had accordingly to be left out. On the other hand, by virtue of its manifold dynamic and rhythmic qualities, the piano affords the great advantage of enabling us to avoid a monotonous uniformity, by varying the harmony of repeated passages or parts. I have endeavoured to make myself clear in the lines set forth, in fact, to obtain a definite form. The few passages in which I considered myself authorised as an artist to add to, or work out the given motives, will easily be found, on comparing my arrangement with the original, written down by Johan Halvorsen.

The above examples from *Slåt* no. 4 (Ex. 11) show firstly Halvorsen's transcription as sent to Grieg (a). The Hardanger fiddle sounds a minor third higher, but Grieg keeps to the key of the notation; the right hand follows Halvorsen fairly closely, but the fifths in the left hand vary the harmonic basis (b). After the *Moderato*, Grieg sees possibilities in the tune for making a contrasting *Tranquillo* section, in which the speed of the melody is halved, and a richer, chromatic, harmonic treatment is possible (c).

Knut Dale was delighted to see his tunes being written down and preserved. But things turned out better than he feared in his letter to Grieg, for the next year his grandson Gunnar Dahle was born. The boy became a splendid player on the Hardanger fiddle, and studied with his grandfather, until the latter's death in 1921. Finally, when Gunnar was about eighty years old, the enterprising Caprice Company recorded him, in stereo, playing a number of the tunes Halvorsen had tried to notate. A record was issued (Caprice CAP 1153) in which these are alternated with Grieg's piano version.

Songs

When Grieg was asked, late in life, why song-writing had comprised such a large proportion of his output, he replied unequivocally that it was due to his wife's singing, and her inspired interpretations – from the earliest days.

> I loved a girl for her golden voice and splendid delivery, and she it is who has been my life's partner to this day. She remains for me, if I may say so, the one true interpreter of my songs.

This, and much other interesting information, comes from a letter of some 6000 words that Grieg sent on 17 July 1900 to the American music critic Henry T. Finck who had requested material for his forth-coming book *Songs and Songwriters*. Grieg made it a strict condition that the letter was to be returned to him and that he was at no time to be quoted in the book as the source of information. Finck honoured this. In the letter Grieg continued by saying that in his early years in Christiania, when his music found little public favour, he settled for enjoying music-making with his wife in the privacy of their own home, or among a circle of close friends.

> My songs of that period all came into being with a sort of natural-law-like necessity, and all were written for her. From that time onward, putting my feelings into songs became a natural necessity like taking breath . . . Her achievement as a singer was my dreamed-of goal as a composer: doing justice to the poem.

Grieg's stated aim as a song-composer is worthy of note, and leads one on to examine *his* part, as opposed to the interpreter's. Undoubtedly his greatest asset here is his abundant melodic gift. In the great majority of his 142 published songs, a memorable tune has been created which conveys the essence of the poem's inner meaning. This will be seen time and time again as the merit of individual songs discussed. Also as he was writing for a practising singer, it is invariably found that these melodic lines are grateful for the human voice.

Grieg's second asset is the accompaniments, which are always attrac-tively laid out for the keyboard player, and which often could stand as piano solos in their own right. Invariably the composer uses his pianistic skill to heighten the meaning of the song both with figuration, and by unfolding effectively his appropriately conceived harmonic support.

Usually the songs make their best impression in the intimate surroundings of domestic music making, for which most were conceived. This can also be cultivated in recordings and broadcast performances. However, in the hands of the right interpreter, concert performances of even the most inward-looking songs can always be effective, as this anecdote, related by Grieg to Finck, shows:

> I was horrified to see *Cradle Song* (Op. 9, no. 2) announced on a Leipzig Gewandhaus programme. Surely unthinkable for concert performance. Let it be said that the singer was Johannes Messchaert, the pianist, Arthur Nikisch. Scarcely had the performance begun when I was struck by the deep hush that descended on the salon. Hope dawned: they were giving a matchless performance. Nor need I have feared. The final notes were succeeded by sustained and thunderous applause from an enraptured auditorium. Those who were present can rarely have heard such glowing depths in *piano* and *pianissimo*, such flawless delivery. As luck would have it the translation was good, too.

This leads on to the main problem in performing Grieg's songs outside Scandinavia: *language*. Few singers can manage the Danish and Norwegian texts, let alone the many very characteristic songs in Landsmål – Norwegian country dialect. Then again, when English audiences do hear the songs in the original Scandinavian languages with the right sounds and the words fitting the vocal melody, the problem is that few understand the meaning. If good English translations of most of the songs were available the problem would be eased. But this is only rarely so. That this *can* be achieved is shown by the English translations of Op. nos. 58, 59, 60 and 61, commissioned by Augener from Lady Macfarren (1828–1916).

This German-born translator and contralto, widow of Sir George Macfarren, principal of the Royal Academy of Music, had the gift of writing sensible English, which fitted Grieg's vocal line, and which approximated to the original. All too often offerings on the market are marred by being translations from German translations (which makes them distant from the original meanings). Or, as a result of the nineteenth-century translator's craze to make all verses rhyme, they need rhythmic alterations in the vocal line; or they completely fail to put over the charm of the Danish and Norwegian poets. One of the worst solutions is that most commonly practised, when English audiences are given performances in the German translations put out by Grieg's Leipzig publisher. Audiences then rarely understand the songs, and the thick German guttural makes a completely different effect from the clear Norwegian and Danish sounds the songs need for their colouring.

If translations are to be used for an English audience, it is far better to use English ones. The audience then gets some understanding of the poem, and English is much closer in sound to Scandinavian languages than is German. There is a considerable need for publication of clear prose translations of all the songs (such as have been achieved for the songs of Hugo Wolf and Schumann in the books on these composers' songs by Eric Sams). There is an even greater need for an enterprising record company to engage a good male and a good female vocalist to record the complete songs, with an accompanying booklet giving original texts printed with line-by-line English translations – similar to the admirable complete recorded edition of Sibelius' songs issued in 1985. Then, at last, the public at large would have a chance to appreciate this treasury of song, whose artistic merit, originality and broad range make it fully worthy of taking its place with the work of other nineteenth-century masters of song-writing: Schubert, Schumann, Brahms, Wolf and Strauss.

The language problem extends to the *titles* of songs. Many variants for one song are found in publishers' lists and artists' concert programmes. In the following discussion of the songs, opus numbers are used liberally. These, while giving a general guide to the publication date of the song, are even more useful as an immutable identification.

When Grieg was a student at the Leipzig Conservatoire, his compositions show that *harmony*, particularly the advanced chromatic techniques of his day, was his main preoccupation. This is seen in the *Four Songs for Alto*, Op. 2, set to German texts and composed in 1861. When he settled in Denmark his interest veered much more to cultivating beautiful melody, and this is seen developing even in the next set of German songs, Op. 4, of 1863–4, where one could cite the plaintive yet charming vocal lines of the little orphan girl in no. 1, and the Aeolian melody of *The Old Song*, no. 5, which is an early example of Grieg incorporating the old church modes into his own style. It had the added advantage here that a medieval colouring was entirely appropriate to the poem. The process of Grieg's melodic development, however, is seen much more strongly in the Danish songs, beginning with the pleasing, but very slight, *Four Romances*, Op. 10, composed in about 1864 (but not published until a few years later and therefore bearing the deceptively high opus number). Then, quite suddenly, the masterpieces of song begin to come.

The manuscript of *Melodies of the Heart*, Op. 5, set to poems by Hans Christian Andersen, is headed 'December 1864' and as Grieg became engaged to his cousin, Nina Hagerup, at Christmas-time, one can look for her inspiration here, particularly in no. 3 of the set, *I love thee*, which became, and has remained, one of the most popular songs ever. It captures, in its tiny length of about one and a half minutes, all the wonder and rapture of a young man's first love, with impassioned, though restrained, excitement. The construction of the song repays careful study, and among the notable features is the diatonic melody, which has just a little chromatic heightening – as with the second note, G sharp. The melody itself also wavers between C major and A minor, which cultivates the mood of unbelieving wonder. Then there is the thrilled fortissimo climax towards which the vocal line grows, and, in the melody's penultimate bar, the A flat, which by changing the leading note of A minor (G sharp) to the flattened sub-mediant of C major (A flat), brings the vocal line to an end, confidently, in C major.

The piano accompaniment is masterly too. The three bars of prelude point the emotional intensity with their subtly used false relations (F natural against F sharp, G natural against G sharp), and these are perfectly balanced by the three bars of postlude resolving all into quiet assurance. The throbbing persistence of the *andante* quavers in almost every bar can also, in the hands of the right pianist, be made entirely appropriate, echoing excited heart-beats.

This song has been examined in some detail because in the listener's enjoyment of such a song there is a natural tendency not to notice the superb craftsmanship which has gone into its making. The manuscript – which can be seen in the Bergen Public Library – as well as the original Danish edition, show that the song was conceived as having one verse. Grieg's Leipzig publishers did him a disservice in issuing their edition in which the whole song is to be repeated to a second verse supplied by the German translator. Why they did this is fairly easy to guess: singers wanted a longer song, but this particular piece does not gain by being doubled in length. Its breathless rapture is much better stated as a miniature, the form in which Grieg excelled. Singers who want a longer piece for performance would do well to perform all four *Melodies of the Heart*. The first of the set, *Two Brown Eyes*, is almost as good. All are short and the Andersen verses give a certain unity to the set. When one thinks of the vast amount of royalties that *I love thee* was to earn in due course, one must be sad for Grieg that he was unable to find a publisher for the Op. 5 songs, and issued them in 1865 at his own expense – when they apparently had few purchasers. 'He is nothing, and has nothing, and writes music no one cares to listen to,' wrote Mrs Hagerup, Grieg's prospective mother-in-law, who was bitterly opposed to her daughter marrying a musician with apparently so few prospects.

Another Andersen masterpiece that followed in 1865 was *The Soldier*, a song showing such a new and unexpected side to Grieg's art, and one of such power and originality that it is amazing that he chose not to publish it. In fact, it only came before the public in 1908 when a collection of ten songs from various stages of Grieg's career were published posthumously by Hansen. The poem, one of Andersen's grimmest, is a dramatic monologue in which the soldier relates with the immediacy of the present tense how his one and only true friend is condemned to die, and is being brought to the place of execution, through the streets, with drums beating. Horror! The soldier himself is ordered to be in the firing squad, and it is his bullet that pierces his friend's heart. Harsh realism is the composer's aim here, the bitter harmonies are of a pungency not equalled anywhere in Grieg's work. The almost complete lack of authentic cadences gives no rest amidst the pounding rhythm of a funeral march that pervades the first part of the song, while tonality seems to dissolve, like life itself, among the increasing dissonances of the last part.

Other highly attractive and melodious settings of Danish poets continued to flow from Grieg's pen in the 1860s. He returned to setting Danish poetry during his friendship with the poet Holger Drachmann in 1886 and 1887, when the two planned their cycle *Travel Memories from Mountain and Fiord*, Op. 44, during a walking tour together in the Jotunheim mountains; and Grieg published other Drachmann settings in his Op. 49. The final sets of Danish songs came in 1900, with Op. 69 and 70, to poems of Otto Benzon.

Grieg was extremely sensitive to texts. Some less-than-good poems, which he set, obviously failed to spark off his inspiration. A number of these were included in the posthumous set published in 1908. Conversely, great poetry would often inspire him to great music, and fortunately a number of Norwegian contemporaries provided him with just what he needed for songs. The first of these was Bjørnstjerne Bjørnson (1832–1910). *From Monte Pincio*, Op. 39, no. 1, was one of Grieg's great achievements, composed with piano accompaniment in 1870, and later published with the accompaniment orchestrated by Grieg, it takes on all the nature of a dramatic and wide-ranging symphonic poem. Bjørnson, contemplating from the nearby mountain, looks out over

Rome. The fast-changing and kaleidoscopic views of the poet are caught by Grieg without any sense of disjointedness, but yet he is able to move convincingly and quickly from the dreamy opening, with its remote introductory chords, to the first verse's rapt melody for the picture of the sunset glow over Rome, to the *più mosso* memories of history, to the *vivo* rhythms of swarming people, and so on. After a vision of future glory for Rome, the song dies away in a haze of distant fragments. This is one of Grieg's longer songs, and he uses the palette of the symphony orchestra's colours to heighten the imagery.

Another notable Bjørnson inspiration are the four *Fisher Lass Songs*, Op. 21. The exquisite melody of no. 1, *The First Meeting*, with its wavering between major and minor, and the gentle arpeggios and ornaments of the piano accompaniment, make it one of the most memorable of Grieg's songs. No. 3, *I give my Song to the Spring*, one of the many pieces in which Grieg responded to this season, captures all its vivaciousness and merriment – provided it is intelligently interpreted, with due care to the many expression marks. A deservedly popular Bjørnson setting is *The Princess*, in which the much-ornamented melody and piano interludes hover over the dominant to create the air of indefinable longing and suspense.

The compressed, cryptic meanings in the poetry of Henrik Ibsen, the other great poet of nineteenth-century Norway, were ideally suited to Grieg's artistry as a miniaturist. The six Ibsen songs, Op. 25, of 1876, deserve to be sung as a set. No. 1 is the highly atmospheric *Fiddlers* whose brooding motif Grieg used in his String Quartet (see below, page 66). The poet's interest in the images of Norwegian folklore are fully matched by Grieg.

No. 2 is *A Swan*, one of the most popular of Grieg's songs, outwardly based on the legend of the swan – silent all its life, but singing at death – yet containing symbolic undertones of a heart's disappointment and distress. The piece makes much the best effect in the short, one-verse format of Grieg and Ibsen, but once again Grieg's German publishers could not resist commissioning their 'translator' to write a second verse, for which the music is to be repeated over again. For a true interpretation of the outer poem, and the inner meaning, a high artistry is called for, and Grieg's copious expression marks have to be carefully followed. The composer orchestrated the piano part, and in this form it makes regular appearances in the concert hall, often being coupled with *From Monte Pincio*. Undoubtedly the accompaniment is enhanced with strings and harp portraying the clear water, and oboe solos suggesting the gliding swan. No. 4, *With a Water-lily*, apart from having a most catching and singable melody, has one of those Griegian accompaniments that, as well as being delightful piano solos in themselves, contain so much of the essence of the song – in this case the waters of the stream. No. 6, *A Bird-song*, is also very melodious and has charming bird-calls echoing in the piano part.

In the two other songs of Op. 25, *Album Verse* and *Departed*, Ibsen's poems tend towards his usual bitterness and often-found preoccupation with disillusioned love, and both are made into masterly miniatures by Grieg. A happier Ibsen song was *Margaret's Cradle Song*, Op. 15, no. 1, whose gentle, warm melody, with its sense of wonder, Grieg conceived soon after the birth of his daughter Alexandra. Ibsen was notoriously difficult to get on with, and had little inclination for music. All the more interesting therefore is Grieg's letter to Beyer from Rome on 19 March 1884, in which he recounts how Nina and he performed at a party, with Ibsen present, nearly all his Ibsen settings. After the songs, wrote Grieg:

> With tears in his eyes he came across to us at the piano and squeezed our hands, almost unable to speak. He mumbled something to the effect that this was real understanding.

Other songs that must be mentioned include Grieg's final set of German songs, Op. 48, which have a more cosmopolitan flavour, and a corresponding widening of emotional range, ending with no. 6, *A Dream*, a favourite and effective concert-hall item; the consistently fine set of six *Elegiac Songs*, Op. 59; and the seven *Children's Songs*, Op. 61. These latter, written to the words of a talented Norwegian schoolmaster, understand the child's world perfectly in ideas and music. They could be used to advantage in English schools, as well as Norwegian, and Lady Macfarren's good English translations are available.

With the songs composed to poems in Landsmål, Grieg identified himself as closely as he could to the perspectives of ordinary Norwegian country folk, though in none of them does he use folk-song. In fact, it cannot be reiterated too strongly that amongst his 142 songs only one (*Solveig's Song*) uses a melody related to folk-song.

The first important writer to use Norway's vigorous, expressive country dialect was the journalist and poet Aasmund Vinje, who had been born of peasant stock and had died in poverty and obscurity in 1870. Grieg discovered his poems shortly afterwards, and used them as the setting for his twelve songs, Op. 33. Most of these are sad in tone, like *Beside a Stream*, in which the poet watches the waters wearing away at the soil covering a tree's roots, so that inevitably the tree will fall, and the poet also reflects on the kisses he had which only brought grief. The grieving beauty of the melody is matched by the pulsating piano part, reminding the listener of the gentle lapping of the brook, but it is the bold and unconventional harmonies that underline the tragedy. In the song *A Broken Friendship*, in which the poet feels all his friends have been false to him, once again biting harmonies bring out the essence of the resigned D minor vocal line. Grieg used two of the Vinje songs, *The Wounded Heart* and *Spring*, for his *Elegiac Melodies* for string orchestra, Op. 34. The grave tone of these two poems, and Grieg's treatment of them, is discussed in the section on orchestral music below (page 83). Some relief is given by *On the Way Home*, whose serene melody matches the comfort the poet finds in the beauties of nature, and the set ends with *The Goal* in which the vigorous and optimistic vocal line praises Landsmål.

The song cycle *Haugtussa*, Op. 67, for soprano (or mezzo), composed 1895 to 1898, is possibly Grieg's greatest achievement in song with piano accompaniment. In the eight sections, the composer selected from a much longer work in Landsmål by the poet Arne Garborg. Grieg takes us deep into the Norwegian countryside among the bilberry slopes and the sparkling streams to experience the emotions of a country girl living remotely in her mountain hut, as she tends the animals on the summer pasture. All is achieved with consummate artistry, with words and music in complete accord. We follow her being lured by a troll, revelling in her herding work in the bright open air, falling in love with a youth from a farm in the valley, being disappointed with his faithlessness, seeking consolation in telling her sadness to the murmuring brook. In every song Grieg uses his melodic gift with unerring psychological insight and sympathy to underline the emotions, while the piano part is a joy throughout, full of mountain effects – whether imitating the gambolling of the kidlings or the ever-changing ripplings of the brook. There is a perfect partnership between soloist and accompanist.

Finally there is the song *The Mountain Thrall*, Op. 32, for baritone and orchestra, composed in Grieg's remote hut at Lofthus in 1878. This has some claim to being considered his greatest work. The poem, in Old Norse, is entitled *Den Bergtekne*, and alternative translations of this, which have gained some currency, include *The Mountain Spell*, *Taken into the Mountains*, *Alone on the Mountainside* and *The Fell Bewitched*. Grieg's Leipzig publishers simplified it into German as *Der Einsame*, and their English edition is translated from this as *Alone* – all of which illustrates the difficulty of rendering Grieg's titles, let alone achieving a consensus on them, in the English-speaking world among publishers, record companies and concert promoters.

Once again Grieg shows himself at his greatest as a miniaturist: the work only lasts six to seven minutes, and the scoring is just for two horns and strings, yet what a depth and power of personal drama it reveals! The poem tells of one who is enticed deep into the mountain forests by elfin maidens, so deep that he feels he is lost forever, and will never discover his way home. He finds it impossible to reach any kind of human relationship with the elves, and a terrible loneliness overwhelms him, and this is made worse when he contemplates the animals and fishes, all of whom have mates. The late 1870s were a lonely time for Grieg, and this is transmuted in this work, which symbolises the loneliness of the artist, who may feel misunderstood by those about him, and who may feel he has lost his way amidst creative problems. In addition, the work reflects in an intense way the relationship of man to Nature, recurringly a preoccupying interest of northern artists.

A brilliantly conceived epigram of two bars opens the piece: for one who has lost his way, what better than to start a piece, whose home key is E minor, with a G minor chord, which gropes its way to the dominant seventh of E? Then the power of the emotions and the darkness of the woods are all symbolised in the way the opening melody is given to two horns, their unison making a most telling effect when a solo horn would have been so much more ordinary. The work has been slower to reach recognition than most of Grieg's works, yet the composer could write to Beyer, with satisfaction, 'I feel as if in this piece I have done one of the few good deeds of my life.'

Choral Compositions

Collaboration with the Norwegian poet, dramatist and novelist Bjørn-stjerne Bjørnson (1832–1910) provided a valuable stimulus to Grieg. Bjørnson was the son of a pastor and spent his boyhood in his father's rural Norwegian parishes before studying at the University of Oslo and taking up work as a dramatic critic. His early novels were concerned with peasant life and a number of them, like *The Fisher Lass* (1868), contained verse-songs of extraordinarily beautiful words. These were followed by a series of plays based on the sagas and early Norse history, which raised him to the front rank among the younger poets of Europe. In 1865 he had been appointed manager of the Christianiä Theatre, writing at first mainly historical plays to produce there. From about 1874, however, his interests completely changed: his busy journalistic work was concerned with radical agitating, and his plays, cast in realistic mould, concentrated on social problems in modern society.

In addition to many songs, both the choral works with orchestra that Grieg published had Bjørnson texts. *Before a Southern Convent*, Op. 20, composed in 1871, was conceived as an opera-scene, and it has in fact been successfully staged, though concert performances have always been much more usual. An exhausted, homeless wanderer from the north (soprano) knocks late at night at the cloister gate, begging for admission. She is questioned by the abbess (alto) about her reasons, and it gradually transpires through her answers that she has witnessed her father being killed by her lover, and although she will love him till death, yet she craves peace away from her native land of storm and cloud. The organ now peals forth from the convent, and a four-part chorus of nuns accompanied by harp welcomes her to where 'grief is abated and the bruised spirit arises to light'. 'I think there is a good deal to be said for dedicating this particular piece to Liszt,' wrote Grieg to Hagen, his Danish publisher – thinking no doubt of how the subject would have appealed to the Abbé Liszt.

The cantata *Landsighting*, Op. 31, for baritone solo, men's choir, orchestra and organ celebrates an episode in the life of Olav Trygvason (AD 964–1000), King of Norway for the last five years of his adventurous life. Olav, as a Viking warrior, had harried the coast of England and France, but he was converted to Christianity by a hermit in the Scilly Isles. He resolved no more to attack fellow Christians, but instead to return to Norway, then still heathen, to convert her people to his new-found faith.

It is at that point that the cantata opens, with an exciting call for the horns, giving the exhilarating feeling of the voyage. Three strophic verses for the choir then follow, describing the voyage, but the orchestra is used to prevent any sense of monotony by providing appropriately different accompaniments for each, and a short interlude after the second verse as the King and his followers search the distant shore of snow-capped mountains and clouds for a suitable landing place. Accompanied by one of Grieg's favourite colouristic devices, achieved by dividing the cellos into four parts, Olav (baritone solo) prays that his faith may 'root as deeply, shine as purely' as the distant mountains. In a final section, the choir echoes Olav's sentiments, their unison lines giving an air of united fervour amid the rich orchestral background now joined by the full sonorities of the organ.

In extolling the art of the miniaturist, Percy Grainger wrote:

> This contraction of emotion and thought into the very briefest of utterances is, in its own very different way, as rare and valuable as the gorgeous expansiveness of German music. To be able to convey deep feeling, fragrance of mood, intense characterisation in two or three chords is a supreme achievement; just as it is another kind of supreme achievement to hold a dominant mood, a central idea unbroken throughout a five-hour opera.

This, aptly, is from Grainger's preface to his English edition of Grieg's *Album for Male Voices*, Op. 30, for in this collection Grieg's art of small-scale mastery reaches one of its supreme achievements. Each of the twelve numbers portrays intense emotions, or sets a mood, or tells a story in the space of a few minutes. Thus the *Children's Song* – with its story of cats banging drums to make the mice dance, and planning to sail down to Denmark so that their paws will not be frozen in the Norwegian winter – is fully as funny in Grieg's realisation as all the humour Wagner generates on a vast scale in *Die Meistersinger*. A complete contrast is provided by *The Great White Host* – a rapt religious meditation, with baritone solo. Its text, part Viking part Christian, imagines a singing throng round God composed of 'heroes who in the world have longed for heaven beyond the grave'.

Notable as Op. 30 is for its imaginative use of Norwegian tunes, its contrapuntal lines leading to daring harmonies, and its novel choral effects, we see all these intensified in Grieg's very last work, the *Four Psalms, freely arranged from Old Norwegian Church Tunes* for mixed choir with baritone solo, Op. 74, composed in 1906. Here we see his art developing into its fullest flowering. Once again we quote from Percy Grainger who was cordially received by Grieg a number of times at Troldhaugen, and who dedicated all his own folk-song arrangements 'lovingly and reverently to the memory of Edvard Grieg':

> On the technical side this last opus carries on the iconoclastic achievements of his *Album for Male Voices*, Op. 30. Both volumes are remarkable for the masterly manner in which highly original and daring complexities of chromatic and enharmonic polyphonic harmony are couched in a perfectly vocal and naturally singable style (through the innate melodiousness of the inner as well as the outer part-writing), thereby, for the first time, making the harmonic innovations of the later nineteenth century available for choral use. It is this side of Grieg's compositional technique (still too little known or appreciated by the musical world at large, though studied and absorbed by modernistic composers with notable results) that has so profoundly influenced modern Anglo-Saxon choral writing. In proving the applicability and effectiveness of post-Wagnerian polyphonic harmonies to and in vocal composition, Grieg has given an impetus to choral music that was lacking throughout the major part of the nineteenth century. Musicians who, in their ignorance of the deepest, most daring and most epoch-making aspects of Grieg's muse, still labour under the delusion that he is mainly a 'simple', 'easy', unsophisticated composer, would do well to study such examples of his highly complex, super-cultivated musical mind as those contained in his Op. 30 and Op. 74.

No. 1, *How fair is Thy Face*, wavers interestingly between minor and major, but this reaches a far higher intensity in No. 2, *God's Son hath set me free*, also to a text by the eighteenth-century bishop Hans Adolf Brorson. The first section is in joyous B flat major. However, Grieg, his musical compositions always reflecting his inmost feelings, writes the middle section with the baritone soloist still singing in B flat major, but the accompanying male four-part choir in B flat minor – a remarkable realisation of the doubts of twentieth-century man (see Ex. 12 overleaf).

Thus, to match the theological questioning, Grieg evolves in this, his last work, the most venturesome development of his harmony, unparalleled in originality among the choral works of the time. The third Psalm, *Jesus Christ our Lord is risen*, to words of Hans Tomisøn, who died in 1573, makes interesting effects with antiphonal writing for a bass soloist alternating with the full choir; while in the fourth, *In Heaven*

(Reprinted by kind permission of Peters Edition, London, Frankfurt and New York.)

above, to words of Laurentius Laurentii (1573–1655), we see the weary composer longing for the final fulfilment of perfect peace.

Grieg's letters make plain that all his life he had seen God in nature, and that through his communing with nature he felt his connection with the divine. 'Before Nature I stood in silent veneration and awe, as before God Himself.' Now, almost at the end of his life, after the increasing ill health of his later years had tormented him almost beyond endurance, he turned to specifically Christian texts to create this remarkable and original church music. The Psalms are possibly Grieg's greatest work. In his diary for 15 September 1906 we read:

Finished three chorales for mixed choir and soloists, a free adaptation from Lindeman's Norwegian Folk Songs. They are so beautiful, these melodies, that they deserve to be preserved in artistic clothing. This small piece of work is the only thing my wretched health has permitted me through all the summer months. This feeling: 'I could, but I cannot' makes one desperate. I fight in vain against heavy odds and must soon give in altogether.

Grieg died, after long periods of insomnia, in Bergen Hospital on 4 September 1907.

Too often in the mid-twentieth century we were treated to shallow estimations of Grieg's art from critics who obviously only know him through a handful of his more popular works. We should always be unwilling to accept an estimate of Grieg as a composer from any critic who does not show a thorough acquaintance with his Op. 30 and 74, as well as, for good measure, the *Slåtter*, Op. 72, and *The Mountain Thrall*, Op. 32. It is only when his most original works, such as these, have been absorbed, that a true appreciation can be reached.

Music for the Stage

In the history of art it is usually found that popular movements in church and state are reflected later in music than in literature and painting. Thus Norwegian nationalism reached a maturity of expression in poetry and drama – particularly in the works of Bjørnson and Ibsen – well before it did so in art-music. It was an advantage to Grieg that these two well-established and inspired writers were there for him to work with. It was also fortunate, as many nineteenth-century Scandinavian composers found, that in their major cities the theatre often alternated opera and drama, so that on drama nights a full orchestra was available, and incidental music required. These circumstances led to the two major commissions Grieg received for theatre music.

The first was for Bjørnson's play *Sigurd Jorsalfar*, based on an episode from the Heimskringla Saga which was to be performed at the Christiania Theatre on 10 April 1872. *Jorsalfar* means 'traveller to Jerusalem', and the whole title is sometimes rendered into English as 'Sigurd the Crusader'. When King Magnus Barefoot died in 1103 he arranged that his three sons Øystein, Sigurd and Olaf should rule jointly. Olaf died young, leaving Norway a dual monarchy. This circumstance gave Sigurd the chance to set off on his pilgrimage (1107–11). On the way he was able to seize considerable treasure from the Moors in Spain, fought against pirates in the Mediterranean, and finally, with his fleet of fifty-five ships, he helped Baldwin I, the Christian King of Jerusalem, to attack and seize Sidon.

The play is principally concerned with the rivalry between the two brothers before Sigurd left Norway. Act I, Scene ii starts with a long monologue by Borghild – the principal female character, and source of intense rivalry between Sigurd and Øystein – and Bjørnson had first asked for music to accompany this:

> Before the curtain goes up, quiet music begins, and as the curtain rises, it depicts Borghild's restless sleep till it reaches a mood of great terror. She cries out, awakes and gets up. The music reflects the confusion and worry.

In the first scene the audience has learned that Øystein has been betrothed to another. Borghild, who loved Øystein, now feels rejected, and swears revenge. Grieg, knowing how difficult it is for an audience to listen to words and music at the same time, rejected Bjørnson's idea of a melodrama. Instead he designed his *Borghild's Dream* as an orchestral introduction, which stops as she begins to speak. The intensity of the music shows the dramatic flair of Grieg the miniaturist. In the drama, Borghild has no sooner finished her soliloquising than Sigurd arrives. There is an emotional meeting between the two, both of whom feel let down by Øystein. Sigurd offers his love to Borghild, and the two ride off together.

In Act II we meet Sigurd and Øystein, surrounded by their followers, in the great hall of the Norwegian Kings. A debate ensues about who is best to be ruler. Sigurd's strength, courage and fighting nature are matched against Øystein's wisdom. To introduce this Grieg provided an orchestral introduction, *The Matching Game*. This had been composed in 1869 as a Gavotte for violin and piano. However, orchestrated it served well – with its contrasting A major and A minor sections – for depicting the characters of the two rival kings: Sigurd, proud and virile, Øystein, milder, weaker, yet still dignified.

Returning to Act II of the play: to everyone's astonishment, Sigurd has Borghild brought in, and demands that she shall decide who is best to be king. She chooses Sigurd. However, he declares he believes his destiny is to go abroad and conquer more lands for Norway, and this he intends to fulfil. He invites the Viking warriors there assembled to join him. For this scene Grieg composed a splendid song given to Sigurd with male chorus, *The Peoples of the North will go forth*, resplendent with the spirit of the old Norse sagas.

In the final Act Sigurd proposes to leave Norway. He seeks out Øystein and tells him how much he believes in him and admires him. The two are reconciled and walk together to the great hall. The *Homage March* is now played by the orchestra and, in its original theatre-form, shows Grieg's dramatic gifts, starting softly with the main tune played and harmonised by four solo cellos – a beautiful and original effect. As more of their followers enter, fuller use is made of the orchestra, and where the stage directions say, 'Here the halberdiers enter in pairs and place themselves on both sides of the steps,' the music, with its leaping bassoon and tuba figures, matches the excitement, which increases further as the two kings are ushered in with fanfares.

Finally, the great thronging Viking host with their shields and spears are depicted, when the full orchestra recapitulates the opening theme, but now *fortissimo* and in augmented notes. (This taut, ever-growing, original version can be seen in the piano-duet arrangement of a selection of his *Sigurd* music that Grieg published in 1874, and which is reprinted in Volume 6 of the new Grieg Complete Edition.) In the great hall there is a lively discussion about what is best: expansion abroad or ploughing the land and revitalising life at home. It is agreed *both* are important, and to conclude the play Grieg sets Bjørnson's *The King's Song* for Sigurd, and male chorus, who praise both Sigurd and Øystein. The short orchestral prelude which Grieg wrote for Act I had been based on this same fervent melody, and now, in its full, glorious, choral form, it makes a magnificent ending, as well as being artistically satisfying in fulfilling what was in the music at the start of the drama.

It is good to have the two choruses, and the four instrumental movements mentioned above, together with horn calls and two further short orchestral interludes, all presented in Per Dreier's recording of the complete *Sigurd Jorsalfar* music.

Both play and music were often performed in Norway, though one wonders how well actors might have been able to sing on occasions. At one early performance Grieg noted that Sigurd was played by a competent actor but when he sang *The King's Song*:

> I had a strong feeling of discomfort, which increased till the pains in my ears were such that I longed to hide myself away, and instinctively bent over more and more.

At this point, Grieg relates, Bjørnson, who was in the next seat, gave him a hefty thump, and said, 'Sit up properly.'

Bjørnson and Grieg next decided to collaborate on an opera, and the poet suggested the idea of Olav Trygvason, whose early career has been noted above, page 41. The libretto was to take up the story from the point where it had ended in *Landsighting*, and was to show heathen Norway, the tremendous impact made by the returning Olav, and the subsequent conversion of the Norwegians to Christianity.

On 10 July 1873 Bjørnson sent Grieg the first three scenes, promising the next by October. The composer liked them and set to work immediately, asking Bjørnson to send at once a synopsis of the whole plot. But no more came from Bjørnson, who went abroad soon after. Then came October and Grieg had to return to his teaching and conducting duties in the capital, hoping that in the next summer he would be able to set to work on the opera again. But the procrastination meant the loss of all momentum for author and composer. On 5 July 1874 Grieg wrote to Bjørnson mentioning that he was composing music for *Peer Gynt*. Bjørnson, thinking mistakenly that this was an opera, flew into a rage. He had been expecting Grieg to join him in the Tyrol to work on the opera; he must have the composer with him, as there might otherwise have to be alteration upon alteration for which he had not got time; Grieg had broken faith. On 12 September Grieg replied:

> If I had actually had your text I should have said no to Ibsen . . . I hope to have finished with this work by autumn (it is only a question of little bits here and there) and will be ready and eager then for *Olav Trygvason*.

Letters trying to arrange a meeting between the two followed, but what suited one did not suit the other. Above all Grieg was delayed throughout 1875 by the *Peer Gynt* music, which he found was taking much more time and trouble than he had envisaged. At last in September he sent the completed score to the Christiania Theatre, the production took place on 24 February 1876, and Grieg wrote again to Bjørnson in a letter of 2 May:

> Don't refuse me what I now beg for. Give me an outline of the plot of *Olav Trygvason* – but soon, at once. Good God, while I write this the longing to buckle down grows to active passion.

But it was too late; Bjørnson had lost interest, and in his own writings had turned away from romantic historical dramas, to plays about social problems in modern Norway. Now followed thirteen years of estrangement between the two, each blaming the other that the opera project was not fulfilled.

In 1889 Grieg made one last attempt to get Bjørnson to complete the libretto, and give him a chance to write the opera he had always craved to compose. But Bjørnson was even less interested, so Grieg decided to orchestrate the three scenes he had completed, and publish them for concert use. The first performance took place in Christiania in October 1889, under Grieg's direction. He used the opportunity to ask Bjørnson to accept the dedication and, by this means, at last healed the rift between them.

The *Scenes from Olav Trygvason* have occasionally been staged, but concert performances have been more usual, a notable English one being that with Norwegian soloists and choirs at the Royal Albert Hall on 28 September 1978.

All three scenes are set in a pagan Norse temple at Trondheim. In the first, of about three minutes' duration, the orchestra at once sets the dark and powerful mood, while the High Priest's recitative invoking the help of Odin and the old Norse gods gives an air of 'long ago' in its Lydian mode. The prominent augmented fourth of the scale, with which each sentence of the recitative ends, acquires increasing intensity as the Lydian mode is transposed up three semitones at each of its subsequent entries. The High Priest's lines are well contrasted with the singing of a woman worshipper who calls on Frigga and the Valkyries for help. Meanwhile the chorus of worshippers gradually gain in importance, from the initial cries of 'Hear us' which punctuate the recitative, to the more animated treatment of 'Other gods are coming, strong and victorious', and then they dominate the stage increasingly with the feelings of strength and confidence radiated for the battle that is about to be waged.

In the second scene, lasting about fourteen minutes, the tempo becomes more agitated as a prophetess, inspired by the old gods, announces that they will meet Olav in the temple. Her part is set firmly in the Phrygian mode, again giving the scene the feeling of great antiquity, while the tremendous crescendi and diminuendi in the orchestra, and the prolonged and bold use of percussion that accompany her incantations, give an atmosphere of stark force, whose weirdness is enhanced by the use of the shrill piccolo. Once again the chorus of Viking worshippers comes more and more to the fore, as they are stirred into expressions of hate for Olav and his new creed, and into a firm and confident resolve to resist him. They echo the prophetess's line that if Olav leaves the temple unscathed, only *then* will they believe him.

The third scene, also of some fourteen minutes, consists of ritual dances to honour the Norse gods, and again the composer conjures up the tremendous fervour of the pagan worshippers of long ago, in the temple lit by sacred fires. The chorus, deployed in a variety of ways, now dominates the action in the round dance, the sword dance, and the great climax that ends the scene.

We must mourn for the Grieg opera that could have been. There are so many good dramatic and musical moments in these scenes, that one can be sure the young Grieg could have achieved a fine full-length work, permeated throughout by his strong melodic gift. The weakness of the work as we have it is that all these scenes are dark in colour and therefore lack the contrast that was always so important to Grieg in his art. But in the full work this could have been rectified by the fourth scene, which would have completed Act I. At a staged performance in Oslo in 1908 the composer's widow said:

I could have wished that at least the closing scene of the act had been completed. The plan was that this act should finish with the remaining behind of the priest's daughter in the temple after the others had gone. When she is about to shut the door, there stands Olav, suddenly, in gleaming armour that shines in the sunlight. Overwhelmed and transported, she falls to her knees before him. With that, the act was to finish.

Olav Trygvason had only to wait a few more years for his exploits in Norway to be set to music, for he is the same as the King Olaf of Elgar's cantata, set to words of Longfellow, and premièred in 1896. Although it was tragic that progress on *Olav Trygvason* was halted, one can only be glad the interruption was occasioned in *Peer Gynt* by a work in which Grieg showed his full powers.

Henrik Ibsen had been born at Skien, Norway, in 1828. When he was eight his father's business failed, and memories of the grinding poverty that ensued are found in *Peer Gynt*. At fifteen he was apprenticed to an apothecary – work that he loathed. He took up writing as a solace, and in 1850 had one play published, and another performed at the Christiania Theatre. In 1851 he was appointed theatre-poet at the new theatre at Bergen founded by the violinist Ole Bull. He held this position until 1857, combining play-writing with work as designer, producer and manager. Work as a theatre manager in Christiania followed, accompanied all the time by prolific literary activities. However, he was dissatisfied with what he felt was the lack of appreciation for his early satires, and when in 1864 the Norwegian parliament refused his application for a state poet's pension, although it had recently granted one to Bjørnson, he left Norway in disgust, living abroad for the next twenty-seven years, mostly in Germany.

It was from here that Ibsen wrote to Grieg on 23 January 1874. He was revising his dramatic poem *Peer Gynt*, composed seven years previously, for a stage production at the Christiania Theatre, and would Grieg undertake the music for it. There followed numerous suggestions, one of which was that the fourth act be replaced by a big tone poem which would depict Peer Gynt's wanderings in the world: 'American, English and French melodies might run as motifs through it, alternating and disappearing.' Finally, Ibsen said he intended to stipulate that the theatre pay an honorarium of four hundred dollars, to be divided equally between author and composer.

Grieg accepted the commission, but not unnaturally expressed his misgivings about some of Ibsen's suggestions for the music. However, on 8 February, Ibsen wrote back, thanking him, and fully agreeing that Grieg must decide how much music to write, and to which scenes.

The deteriorating financial position of Grieg's parents had forced them to sell their home at Landås near Bergen, where Grieg had found peace for work during many previous summers. Now, having this year relinquished his teaching and conducting duties in Christiania, Grieg and his wife were living in lodgings in Bergen. He found it impossible to work there, but fortunately a well-to-do local businessman, Rolfsen, lent him a one-room pavilion in a secluded position with broad views of sea and woodland. Much of the *Peer Gynt* music was written there. But it took considerably longer than Grieg had imagined. In a letter from The Pavilion to Beyer of 27 August he said:

> With *Peer Gynt* it goes very slowly . . . it is a frightfully intractable subject, with the exception of one or two parts, as for example where Solveig sings — all of which I have done.

The next day he wrote to Ludwig Josephson, director of the Christiania Theatre:

> I was glad to learn from your letter that the first performance of *Peer Gynt* will not take place till 1875, because it would have been impossible for me to have had the music ready for the earlier date. The task is much greater than I had thought and in some places I come up against difficulties that bring me to a standstill. But I hope by the end of the year to have it finished.

Grieg remained completely engrossed with the music for a great deal longer than that, and it was only in September 1875 that he at last sent the full score to the theatre. Even then there followed a long letter on 14 December to Hennum, the conductor of the theatre's orchestra, in which Grieg detailed a number of changes to be made in the orchestration and asked him to make the corrections in score and orchestra parts. More interestingly the letter continues:

> The music is only music in the fewest instances: it ventures out on thin ice to caricature and characterise often in such a coarse manner that it is essential to achieve precisely the effect which will make the public understand its meaning.

Grieg then wrote notes about the 25 items in the full score at that time, and how they were to be interpreted.

It is gratifying to learn that after their two years of labour the first performance of the play with Grieg's music on 26 February 1876 was a great success for author and composer (though neither were present); and 35 more performances followed during the season.

But Grieg was far from finished with *Peer Gynt*; he was constantly revising the music or adding new numbers for later performances. Thus he wrote to Beyer on 5 January 1886 before a new production in Copenhagen:

> I am hard at it with *Peer Gynt*, which I am re-orchestrating . . . In the café I am bombarded by music copiers and music directors who snatch the score from me sheet by sheet as soon as I have them ready.

Soon after the Copenhagen production Grieg wrote to his Leipzig publishers saying that he did not think a production of *Peer Gynt* in Germany was a likelihood, therefore he was going to prepare an edition for concert use. There followed the two suites for orchestra in 1888 and 1891. Then in 1908, a year after the composer's death, Peters published a full score containing 23 numbers. This included an orchestration of Grieg's piano piece *The Wedding Procession passes by* – undertaken by Halvorsen with the composer's agreement, for production at the Christiania National Theatre, when he was there as conductor. But at least another six pieces of *Peer Gynt* music survive in manuscript. How wrong too Grieg was about a production of *Peer Gynt* in Germany! The first performance in Berlin took place in 1913. Mrs Nina Grieg was there as a guest of Kaiser Wilhelm. With Grieg's music it was presented in two Berlin theatres simultaneously, achieving 1000 performances. Performance in more than 50 German theatres followed.

It is only reasonable to suppose that many of the public who flocked to hear its performances in Germany, France, Britain and the USA did so because they knew Grieg's music, and were keen to find out what adventures befell Solveig, Anitra, Ingrid and the others to call forth this lovely music.

Grieg felt that in extracting eight items for his two orchestral suites he had published all that was suitable for concert use, and it is certainly true that most of the other numbers are far too short or far too slight to stand on their own. On the stage though it is a different matter; many give, in a few bars, just the right amount of mood setting, or under-lining of a satirical or poetic moment in the text that will make the whole more effective. Undeniably, though, Grieg was more successful in giving musical expression to the parts of the play that suited his muse – particularly the romance and the Norwegian folklore. With the bitter and satirical elements, the faithlessness, the selfishness, the irresponsibility, the futility of much of Peer's character, he had little sympathy. It is these last-named elements that have interested mid-twentieth-century theatre producers much more, and thus Grieg's music has often been jettisoned from modern productions so that the harshness of Ibsen's drama can make its full impact. Another alternative has been to use Harald Saeverud's incidental music of 1947 which, ably and effectively written, is much more 'realistic'.

It may be of help to readers who do not know Ibsen's play if some of its main actions are now sketched, with an indication of how the music fits in, for in modern recordings it is quite usual for the pieces to be presented not in the form of the two suites which Grieg published, but in the sequence of the drama.

Peer Gynt is a lying, boasting, irresponsible, selfish, drunken ne'er-do-well. But he has a perky energy and complete optimism about his own future affairs, and this is caught up in his own motif, with which the Prelude opens (Ex. 13):

Ex.13

Solveig's motif, first shyly, then more intensely, makes its appearance, and the playing of a country fiddler is heard 'as if from afar'. The third section develops the opening theme in a way that reminds us of all the adventures, real or imaginary, of which the young Peer boasts, and its concluding figures, bantered between high and low instruments, make a perfect introduction for the opening scene – in the impoverished family farm where Peer's widowed mother Åse, who had sent him out to hunt for food, reproaches him for coming back with none, and losing his gun as well. Peer counters with a wild story, of how he stunned a reindeer, but it jumped up, pinning him against its back with its antlers, and carried him across glaciers and mountain tops.

Hearing how Ingrid, a former girl-friend, is to be married to another lad, Peer sets off for the wedding, uninvited. A peasant fiddler plays for the dancing, and at the festivities Peer is attracted by Solveig, the young daughter of newcomers to the district; but his wildness frightens her, and the other villagers have no time for Peer, dressed in rags, and soon drunk. Suddenly, all are aghast. Peer Gynt has made off with the bride, and can be seen in the distance carrying her higher and higher up the mountainside.

Act II is introduced by an orchestral prelude (entitled in suite No. 2 *The Abduction of the Bride and Ingrid's Lament*). Grieg wrote to Hennum:

> It is absolutely vital the contrasts are emphasised, since different characters are presented here; Ingrid, *andante*, who laments imploringly towards the end, even threateningly; and Peer Gynt, *allegro furioso*, telling her to get the hell out of it.

Peer has seduced Ingrid on the mountainside, and now abandons her, despite her entreaties. Atmospheric music, with singing and melodrama, next comes for an extended scene in which Peer flirts with three herd girls, living in their *saeter*, or huts, to tend the animals on the mountain pastures.

The villagers are out in angry mood searching for Peer. He runs in distraught, accidentally strikes his head against a rock and falls stunned. He dreams he meets a Woman in Green, engages her in amorous conversation. It turns out she is the Troll King's daughter. Peer poses as the 'son of Queen Åse', and they set off for the King's hall – a cavern deep in the Dovre mountains.

The famous movement, included in the first suite, ensues. Built entirely out of one motif constantly repeated, constantly varied, it is a remarkable study in crescendo and accelerando, generating enormous excitement and frenzy (Ex. 14).

Ex.14

'The bass drums and cymbals must thunder as much as the fabric can take,' wrote Grieg to Hennum. In the original, amid wild dancing, a chorus of trolls, enraged that Peer should want to marry their princess, advance more and more threateningly on him demanding his blood. However, the Troll King silences them and asks his daughter to dance. Grotesque music follows, reminding us that the trolls are uncouth and evil goblins. Pressed for a comment, Peer says the spectacle was unbelievably ugly, and the incensed trolls set on him to more wild music. Church bells sound from the valley, the trolls vanish with shrieks and Peer awakes from the nightmare. He next sends a message to Solveig, imploring her not to forget him.

Act III is ushered in with a tiny atmospheric prelude for strings and horns, entitled *In the Depths of the Pine Forest*. Peer is building a small wooden house. Solveig, having left her family, comes to join him. Peer feels he must go out into the world to prove himself, and bidding Solveig to wait for him, sets off. He first visits his mother's home, and finds her in bed dying. Trying to cheer her up he pretends the bed is a cart, and he is driving it to take her on a celestial journey. He launches into a cheery monologue but all the time the deeply moving and tragic music underlines the pathos, and tells us that Åse's life is ebbing away, and before its last sombre bars are reached, Peer realises his mother is already dead.

The heavenly movement *Morning Mood*, so fresh, so clear, which Grieg used to open the first suite, serves as prelude to Act IV. 'I imagine the sun breaking through the clouds at the first *forte*,' Grieg told Hennum. After years of wandering, Peer is now in Morocco, a wealthy tycoon, the owner of a yacht lying at anchor. But he quarrels with four business associates, who, in his absence, make off in his yacht, leaving Peer penniless.

Next Peer, who has stolen a horse and magnificent robes, is seen surrounded by Arab girls who hail him as the returning Prophet (*Arabian Dance* of the second suite). One of the girls, Anitra, particularly takes his fancy, but she tricks him out of his purse of gold and rides away on his horse, leaving Peer penniless again. At this moment he sees a vision of Solveig waiting for him in Norway, singing her famous song of hoping and loving and longing for his return.

Eventually Peer turns for home, wealthy again, elderly and still as cynical as ever. But as his ship nears the coast of Norway it sinks, with all his possessions, in a violent storm. (This is the music for the third movement of the second suite.) So Peer returns to Norway as empty-handed as he left it. However, Solveig, now nearly blind, welcomes him. He asks her what has been the reality of his existence all these years, where was he? Solveig answers, 'In my faith, in my hope, in my love.' Peer sinks down in her arms and, as the sun rises across the mountains, the play ends with her lullaby, which Grieg sets as a wonderful poem of true love.

Chamber Music

Grieg's chamber music raises the problem of his relationship to sonata-form. He was working in an age when the musical intelligentsia and critics were prone to assess a composer's capabilities by his handling of this form, which usually meant comparing the newcomer's works to those of the German masters such as Haydn and Beethoven. Sonata-form, with its careful system of formal and tonal balance, had grown out of eighteenth-century composers' response to the Age of Reason. There is no denying that it admirably suited the expression of composers such as Haydn and Mozart. Beethoven too was able to realise new possibilities in the form so that the development sections in particular suited his genius for working with small, pregnant motifs.

However, as the nineteenth century continued, Romantic composers had to face the dilemma of whether to give priority to their poetic ideas or to the demands of form, and it became an increasingly difficult problem for them. The early Romantics such as Schubert and Mendelssohn gave priority to their melodies, but a certain classical restraint still enabled them to accommodate sonata-form for many successful instrumental and orchestral works. On the other hand, one finds the wild, free genius of the young Schumann fashioning new forms for his most successful early large-scale works, like his *Carnaval*, Op. 9, and *Fantasia*, Op. 17, and with Liszt's *Faust* and *Dante* Symphonies of the 1850s, symphonic form takes a very subservient place behind the programme of the music.

Sonata-form, as left by Beethoven, was not really congenial to Grieg's genius, and yet he felt compelled to work at it in order to win prestige in the European, and particularly German, musical circles of his day. Twice he shut himself away from the world 'determined to fight my way through the great forms, cost what it may'. The first time he had sufficient financial resources to do this was in 1877–8, when he had a work hut erected at Lofthus on the Sørfiord, an arm of the Hardanger fiord. The String Quartet resulted. But the other chamber works Grieg hoped would follow did not – though other masterpieces written there that year included *The Mountain Thrall* and the *Album for Male Voices*.

Again in 1882–3, with a cash advance from Peters, commissioning a second piano concerto, Grieg shut himself away. But he was not able to solve his problems of form as he had been able to do in his youth, fourteen years earlier, and the second concerto never evolved beyond a few sketches. However, the cello sonata resulted from the year's labours.

After that Grieg only once more completed a work in sonata-form – the Violin Sonata no. 3 of 1887.

With Grieg's five chamber music works, instead of looking in them for interesting handling of sonata-form, as the German critics of the day did, or comparing them with Brahms's output of the same period, it is wiser to take them as original works in their own right. For Grieg, the lyricist, sonata-form offered at its very simplest a convenient framework in which to display a number of poetic ideas. Thus, in the slow movements with their middle section; in the dance movements with their trios; and in the outer movements with their first and second subjects, many ideas could be presented. It was this very richness of melodic material – with the first and second subjects often consisting of whole groups of themes – that the academic critics of the day found disturbing and unsuitable to sonata-form, as they construed it.

Grieg told Bjørnson in 1900 that he thought his three Violin Sonatas were among his best works: 'They represent periods in my development – the first naïve, rich in ideas; the second national; and the third with a wider horizon,' and in his lifetime they became extremely popular both on the concert platform, and among the large numbers of amateur musicians, who wanted attractive music to play at home which was not too technically difficult. It is interesting to see the rave reviews that Grieg's music regularly received in the late nineteenth and early twentieth centuries, and a random sample for each of the violin sonatas is reproduced below to show the kind of effect his music had on contemporaries:

Frederick Niecks (later to be Professor of Music at Edinburgh University, but at the time of writing, in 1879, a lecturer in music there) on the first Violin Sonata:

> It calls up in our imagination scenes such as the composer was surrounded by in his youth – the sea-port town leaning against high mountains of rock, the Byfjord, and the main beyond. We are in the open air with a bracing breeze about us. Amid these invigorating influences that dilate the whole being, body and soul, the meaning of the interval of the ninth at once reveals itself. The interval of the eleventh, which occurs in the second bar of the first subject, is only a more potent interpreter of the same feeling. Smoothly the boat glides onward, the water rushing and splashing along its sides. Now we are in the open sea, a wide expanse bounded only by the horizon . . . The remaining portion of the working-out section pictures the whistling

and roaring of the storm, the upheaving of the waves, the creaking and groaning of the vessel . . . The first movement tells us of the action and the struggle with the elements.

Gerhard Schjelderup (a Norwegian composer who published a biography of Grieg in 1903) on the second Violin Sonata:

> The first Sonata is the work of a youth who has seen only the sunny side of life, while the second is the gift to the world of a man who has learned to shiver in the cold mists of night, and has learned the meaning of grief and disappointment.
> The tragic nature of his home overwhelms the artist. For this reason the second sonata is in a deeper sense much more Norwegian even than the first; for a Norway without tragedy is not a complete Norway, but only a part of the varied impressions which this mighty dreamland gives to him who can understand the language of nature.

Ernest Closson (Belgian musicologist at the Conservatoire of Brussels, who in 1892 published a booklet *Edvard Grieg and Scandinavian Music*) on the third Violin Sonata:

> It must be classed with the most inspired scores ever written. It is, in our opinion, the work of Grieg which most truly deserves to be called grand. From beginning to end it is a marvel of inspiration, intelligence, independence. Finally, there is, what contributes not a little to the grandeur just referred to, a simplicity, an austerity, a sort of classicism within modernity in the final movement. Had Grieg composed nothing but this sonata it would suffice to hand his name down to posterity.

In the anti-Romantic mid-twentieth century, accolades like this for the Violin Sonatas were rare. However, hearing them again in the late twentieth century, when mercifully it is more usual to accept works on their own terms, listeners can again be struck by the freshness and originality they exuded in their time. Whatever we may think of Niecks' credentials for reviewing the work, we should surely heed Franz Liszt when he wrote to Grieg after being shown the first Violin Sonata:

Rome, 29 December 1868

Sir,
I am glad to be able to tell you of the sincere pleasure that I have derived from reading through your Sonata, Op. 8. It bears witness to a talent for composition – vigorous, reflective, inventive, and of

excellent material – which has only to follow its own way to rise to the heights. I assume that in your own country you receive the success and encouragement that you deserve. These will not be lacking for you elsewhere either: and if you come to Germany this winter, I warmly invite you to visit Weimar for a while, so that we may get to know each other.

Franz Liszt.

Among other things, Liszt would have been struck by the strange effect of the opening sustained chords of E minor and A minor, which make the first subject, which immediately follows, so exciting (Ex. 15):

Ex.15

but perhaps he had never before heard effects like those in the middle movement where Grieg imitates the Hardanger fiddle (see Ex. 16 overleaf):

Ex.16

Grieg's melodic fount flows very freely in all movements, and although the weakest parts are the development sections of the outer movements, the unconstrained rhythms of wind and waves in the first always sustain the interest. The first performance was given in November 1865 in the Gewandhaus, Leipzig, by the Swedish violinist Anders Petterson with the composer at the piano, and the same month Peters printed a cautious first edition of 125 copies.

The second Violin Sonata, dedicated to Johan Svendsen, was composed in July 1867 and first performed the following autumn at an Edvard Grieg Evening in Christiania, with the solo part played by Gudbrand Böhn and the composer at the piano. Grieg, as we have seen, regarded it as more 'national' than the first. This is achieved partly by the lively Norwegian dance rhythms that inform some of the subjects, and also by the much darker harmonic colouring. The sunny beech woods of Denmark are exchanged for the dark pine forests of Norway, for which the free rhapsodic opening sets the tone.

Perhaps because of this 'nationalism', even less attempt than usual is made to provide development sections: that in the first movement is short and weak while the finale does not have one at all. Another structural weakness lies in the main themes of the last movement, which are too reminiscent of what has gone before to provide a strong ending. The first subject is similar to that in the first movement, and the second main melody in E flat reminds one of the middle section of the middle movement — in both cases, one feels, accidentally.

The mood of the Violin Sonata no. 3 in C minor, Op. 45, composed at Troldhaugen in the autumn of 1886 and finished there the following January, is predominantly tragic. This time the composer is more than usually successful in using sonata-form to show off his material to advantage; thus the first movement's first subject (Ex. 17(a)), with which the work opens, makes an interesting main point of the development section when, over a harp-like accompaniment and a bass descending in semitones, it is presented in augmentation (Ex. 17(b)):

Ex.17

Finally, it generates the coda. The powerful treatment the first subject receives in the development section gives plenty of interest, and Grieg, therefore, wisely did not introduce into it the delicate, melodious second subject. However, in this latter, the Griegian method of taking the first two bars of a melody and elaborating them in bars three and four, which are then in turn expanded to an eight-bar phrase, seems here entirely suitable to sonata-form (Ex. 18):

Ex.18

The long, heavenly melody of the second movement in E major, presented first by the piano and next by the violin, is followed by an anxious middle section, and is most interestingly recapitulated because its first eight bars appear in E flat major, and only then does it glide back to E major, with a great feeling of a goal achieved and classical symmetry appeased. The last movement is again interesting in that, although there is no development section as such, the first and second subjects are considerably developed in the course of the movement. Thus the first subject has a powerful continuation and generates a *Prestissimo* coda, while the second subject, which was rather subdued on its appearance in the exposition, is recapitulated in a far more brilliant and rhythmically lively form.

The première of the third Violin Sonata took place in the Neues Gewandhaus in Leipzig on 10 December 1887, with the composer partnered by the Russian violinist Adolph Brodsky (1851–1929). Bernsdorf, in Germany's most influential musical journal *Signale*, gave the Sonata a damning review but elsewhere, all over Europe and North America, it was acclaimed as a masterpiece.

The Cello Sonata in A minor, Op. 36, was written for, and dedicated to, the composer's cellist brother, John Grieg (1840–1901), and the manuscript in the Bergen Public Library is marked 'completed 7 April 1883'. During the years Grieg was conductor of the Bergen Symphony Orchestra (1880–2) he gave a number of chamber music recitals with his brother, both in Bergen and in other Norwegian towns. Possibly this close association with a cellist and his instrument resulted in the very idiomatic writing we find here, with the cello's full resources exploited (it is not one of those works in which the cello lingers over the 'A' string almost all the time); and the main subjects are long-breathing melodies, which emanate from the soul of the instrument.

Grieg had usually relied on a wealth of themes to carry him through sonata-form movements up to this date (see for example the Overture *In Autumn* or the String Quartet), however in the Cello Sonata he quite deliberately seemed to be planning to have fewer themes and to use them more diversely. Thus the first subject's opening three minims (E, F, E) are exploited into a motif of three reiterated notes, which constantly reappear to drive the music along; and the first subject is also used to make a C major link passage to usher in the second subject. The first subject also generates the coda. A successful innovation in form is provided by the cello cadenza towards the end of the development section: the second half of the cadenza is accompanied, and it merges imperceptibly into the recapitulation.

The second part of the coda – *Prestissimo* – is among a number of features of this Sonata which remind one of Grieg's Piano Concerto in the same key (in this case of the Concerto's opening). The noble melody of the second movement's opening will also remind the listener of the *Homage March* from *Sigurd Jorsalfar*, though in the Sonata it is marked to be played much more slowly. This gives time for the grandly arpeggiated piano accompaniment to its second statement, as well as the richly chromaticised recapitulation, to make their effect. The triplet figure in the main subject is used to form the basis of the more agitated middle section, as well as for the *tranquillo* closing page.

Grieg tries to move even closer to the monothematic devices of Schumann (as for instance exemplified in the latter's Fourth Symphony) in his finale, when the first subject in A minor is transferred into a second subject, by being transposed up to C major, with its notes augmented to twice their former length. But this kind of symphonic transformation was not Grieg's strong point, and a certain amount of monotony results. However, the work is a useful and attractive item in the cello repertoire, and after the first performance at Dresden on 22 October 1883, in which the German cellist and composer Friedrich Grützmacher was partnered by Grieg, it became extremely popular.

Grieg's sketchbook in the Bergen Public Library has four amusing drawings of about twenty villagers erecting his work hut for him by the fiord at Lofthus. In the last one the hut is in position, Grieg has bought a large barrel of beer, and all are celebrating, while a folk-fiddler plays. The hut can still be seen there – in the grounds of the Hotel Ullensvang – slightly moved from its original position, but enjoying similar views of the fiord, the towering mountains and the tremendous water-fall cascading down the fell side. It was here that he composed his String

Quartet in G minor, Op. 27, at a time, he said, when he sought rest in the country after heart-rending experiences.

He never elaborated on what these were, but it is at least possible that the song *Spillemaend* (Fiddlers), Op. 25, no. 1, which provides the main and ever-brooding motif of the Quartet, may provide a clue. The text, by Ibsen, tells of a musician who spends every night of the summer thinking of his beloved, from whom he is separated. Wandering alone by a stream he wonders if the water-sprite could teach him a magic song that would impel his fair one to return to him. But it is too late. She has given his brother her love. He wanders, playing, in palaces and great halls; but a tempest of terror plays in his heart.

Possibly a temporary difficulty in Grieg's marriage was the starting point for the emotional experience in the Quartet. Certainly Nina Grieg did not accompany her husband to Lofthus, 1877–8, when the composer had lodgings at a farm and spent the day working in his hut by the fiord. That we are justified in looking to the song for biographical influences in the Quartet is shown by Grieg's letter of 8 January 1897 to the conductor Iver Holter. After copying out the first part of Ibsen's poem, the composer says this is the song he quotes from in his Quartet.

And herein lies, as you will understand, a bit of a life story, and I know I had to endure a great spiritual struggle and I expended a great deal of spiritual energy in giving shape to the first part of the Quartet there among the dark mountains of the Sørfiord in the sweet summer and autumn.

But whatever the emotions in Grieg's heart at the time, they are transmuted in the Quartet into universal ones of sadness and anger, always set, as is Grieg's way, in the context of the healing open-air world of nature. We see this particularly in the third movement, *Intermezzo*, in which the lofty and careworn emotions of the solitary composer are contrasted with the movement's middle section – a lively country-dance, into which the four instruments plunge, one after the other.

The first four bars of the Ibsen song (Ex. 19):

Ex.19

som — mer lys nat,
her *I* *dream*

(which also appear in the minor mode in the song's fourth verse) give
rise to the main motif of the Quartet, played at the very opening in its
brooding, minor form (Ex. 20):

Ex.20

This in turn, in a major form, becomes the first theme of the second
subject (Ex. 21):

Ex.21

Here one sees Grieg's favourite method of melodic elaboration: bars
six to seven are expanded in bars eight to nine and then again in bars ten
to eleven. The motif also generates a subsidiary theme, and the *Presto*
coda of the first movement. The pastoral reveries of the slow movement
are three times interrupted by an *Allegro agitato* theme derived from it.
Again the motif haunts the main theme of the *Intermezzo* (Ex. 22):

Ex.22

It opens the finale in its minor form, and ends it, with a sudden burst of anxious hope, in its major form.

The emotional and musical unity given by Grieg's song motif is enhanced by the figure (a), the Grieg motif, which gives a structural unity by appearing in themes of all four movements.

The Grieg quartet was extremely novel at its time in abandoning the traditional contrapuntal style of quartet writing for a style based firmly on melody and harmony. Also the frequent double-, triple- and quadruple-stopping for the stringed instruments, which was necessary for Grieg to achieve his desired harmonic richness, caused surprise in purist chamber music circles, and were probably the main reason why Dr Abraham, director of Peters, refused the work. Earlier, hearing Grieg was at work on a quartet, he had said Peters would be interested in publishing it, but on receiving the score in the summer of 1878, he sent it back to the composer, suggesting he rework it as a piano quartet or a string quintet. As it stood, it was almost unplayable.

Terribly upset by this rebuff, Grieg wrote to Robert Heckmann in Cologne, who with his Quartet was planning to give the first performance that October. 'Is he right?' he asked. Heckmann, who had been enthusiastically rehearsing the Quartet, wrote back:

> In the presence of my colleagues in the quartet . . . I hasten to say that in our unanimous opinion there is not the slightest reason for rewriting your work either as a piano quartet or a string quintet. The sound effects in all the four movements are characteristic of, and designed for, string instruments rather than the piano . . . it would be a pity if the quartet were to lose its present sonority and characteristic form.

Heckmann's Quartet gave the first performance at Cologne on 29 October 1878 in an all-Grieg programme, in which the composer also played his Piano Sonata, and partnered Heckmann in the second Violin Sonata. At Grieg's particular request a group of his songs was also included in the programme, but *Spillemaend*, most interestingly, was not among them. Grieg obviously did not want to publicise any link between its text and the Quartet but wished, rather, that the Quartet should stand independently as a work in its own right.

Heckmann's Quartet followed this performance with others in many German cities. After the one at Leipzig on 30 November, Bernsdorf's venomous review in *Signale* was regarded by Dr Abraham as ample justification for his refusal to publish it. However, it was from this very winter that Grieg's music began, quite suddenly, to be popular in Germany. The Quartet played its part, and it is amusing to find that a few years later Dr Abraham, who now wanted the Quartet for Peters' list, had to pay a handsome price for the rights to E. W. Fritsch, the small German publishing house who had enterprisingly brought it out in 1879. From that time on he realised that, whatever the critics and his staff advisers said, the public wanted Grieg's music, and he never again refused a Grieg composition.

It is interesting to note Franz Liszt's continuing appreciation of Grieg's art. In October 1879, Heckmann wrote to Grieg that he had performed the Quartet in Wiesbaden. Liszt had been in the audience and said:

> It is a long time since I heard a new composition, particularly a string quartet, which has interested me as much as this unusual and brilliant work of Grieg's.

And Liszt also said he was planning to promote performances in Weimar and Rome.

Grieg was present at a performance of the Quartet in Rome in 1884, and from his letter home to Beyer we get a glimpse of the popular acclaim that was now greeting him and his music throughout Europe:

> When the first movement was finished, the audience broke into applause which was simply endless. Can you understand such a thing? The Italians, with a piece like that! . . . the whole audience had risen and turned to face me, and up on the platform the players joined in the clapping. One's own innermost soul expressed in the scenery of Hardanger finding its way straight to Italian hearts – it's unbelievable!

In his hut at Lofthus, in 1878, Grieg attempted to compose one more chamber work – a Trio for violin, cello and piano. Only the Andante was completed. This sonata-form movement in C minor, of some nine minutes' duration, expresses, as does the Quartet, the composer's innermost thoughts against the background of mountains and fiord. Unusually for Grieg, the melodious second subject is derived from the first, which contributes to the tautly organised, flowing structure. It certainly deserves an occasional performance, and after lying in manuscript for 100 years, has now been published, and achieved its first UK broadcast on Christmas Eve, 1985.

How then are we to summarise Grieg's achievement in the five chamber works he published? The talent of the composer is certainly much more richly displayed in the poetic ideas than in handling *form*. However, the weakness of the latter is easily outweighed by the advantages of the former, as Tchaikovsky pointedly asserts in an entry about Grieg in his *Diary of my Tour Abroad in 1888*:

Hearing the music of Grieg, we instinctively recognise that it was written by a man impelled by an irresistible impulse to give vent by means of sounds to a flood of poetical emotion, which obeys no theory or principle, is stamped with no impress but that of a vigorous and sincere artistic feeling. Perfection of form, strict and irreproachable logic in the development of his themes, are not perseveringly sought after by the celebrated Norwegian. But what charm, what inimitable and rich musical imagery! What warmth and passion in his melodic phrases, what teeming vitality in his harmony, what originality and beauty in the turn of his piquant and ingenious modulations and rhythms, and in all the rest what interest, novelty, and independence!

For Orchestra

Grieg evolved a highly personal form of orchestration, which is undeniably effective for his music. 'Evolved' is the key word because his characteristic style was only perfected after he had had time for further study in the 1880s, and above all after he had had considerable experience as a conductor – of the Bergen Symphony Orchestra from 1880–2, and as a guest conductor of leading European symphony orchestras on frequent concert tours to Germany, France, England and Holland. However, almost all his published orchestral works bear this maturity of style, because early works like the Overture *In Autumn*, Op. 11, and the Concerto, Op. 16, were re-scored before publication of their definitive editions in the later part of his career.

The Griegian style aims above all to give clear, bright presentation of the melodies. Thus we find in his scores many woodwind solos for piccolo, flute, oboe, clarinet and bassoon. These are rarely doubled at the unison, which would submerge their distinctive colours. String melodies, on the other hand, are often doubled at the unison in effective combinations (for example, solo cello with violins, or violins with violas) to enhance the strength of the line, and also often appear doubled in octaves, or in three octaves.

The warm colours of the horns stand out prominently in some works like *In Autumn* and many *Peer Gynt* movements, but the other brass instruments are held much more in reserve. Many of Grieg's scores include three trombones and tuba in the instrumentation, though he rarely uses these lower brass instruments to make a rich harmonic texture as Wagner did. They and the trumpets are mostly used to heighten climaxes and accentuate chords, and in both cases the characteristic Griegian method is to use them *staccato* as, for instance, in *In the Hall of the Mountain King*, where the parts for these six instruments are *staccato* throughout.

The percussion too is used sparingly (except in *In Autumn* where the conductor needs to restrain the somewhat exuberant use of cymbals and bass drum or they can be counter-productive). Triangle, tambourine and side drum usually only make their appearance where deliberately exotic effects are called for, as in works like *Anitra's Dance*, and *Arabian Dance*. It is interesting to see that in the early editions of the Piano Concerto, the timpani's opening one-bar roll is doubled by two horns. Here too Grieg came to prefer the primary colour of the timpani alone, and in later revised editions the horns' part is deleted.

Care is also given in Griegian scoring to presenting the harmonies richly, yet never in a way that will detract from the melody. For this he relies heavily on effective methods of dividing string sections into two, three or four parts. A large body of strings is needed for almost all Grieg's works, including those for strings alone, to make the various gradations of *divisi* writing effective.

In harmonic blocks of sound, Grieg was fond of contrasting lower strings with upper strings, or the woodwind section with the string section (there are a number of felicitous examples in *Morning Mood*); and we find much less mixing of colours than was usual with his con-temporaries. The blended hues Wagner cultivated throughout Act I of *Parsifal* were the opposite of Grieg's method. For him bright, primary colours were the order of the day.

In the earliest surviving orchestral work – the Symphony in C minor – we find that the twenty-year-old Grieg, although he had learned to score reasonably competently at the Leipzig Conservatoire, had developed only a few of the characteristics that were to distinguish him as a mature orchestrator.

The history of Grieg's Symphony is one of the strangest. In the spring of 1863 he had gone to live in Copenhagen, looking forward, among other things, to the chance of meeting Niels W. Gade (1817–90), the foremost Danish composer of the day. Gade's *Echoes of Ossian* Overture, Op. 1, with its dark, northern colours, had been received as an interesting and promising novelty in Denmark and Germany in 1841. In 1843 Gade sent Mendelssohn the manuscript of his First Symphony, which he had been unable to get performed in Denmark. Mendelssohn promptly conducted the première in Leipzig and, when Gade arrived there, engaged him to be deputy conductor of the Gewandhaus Orchestra. There followed friendship with Schu-mann, who based his *Northern Song* (Op. 68, no. 41) on the notes G A D E. The northern features of Gade's early music were soon sub-merged in his later symphonies and concertos by the tides of German romanticism and, interestingly, Grieg wrote that he 'wanted to be-come personally acquainted with this significant artist who knew how to give his thoughts such a masterly and clear form' – rather than men-tioning any 'northernness' in Gade. *Form* and *competence* there certainly were in Gade's music.

When the two men were introduced by Matthison-Hansen, the Danish composer, Gade asked Grieg if he had any compositions to show him. Grieg gave a negative response, feeling his early works were not good enough. 'Then go home and write a symphony,' said Gade. Within fourteen days Grieg had composed and orchestrated the first movement. Gade was pleased with it and urged Grieg to continue. The manuscript records that it was completed on 2 May 1864. The last three of the four movements were performed at a public concert in the Tivoli Gardens in Copenhagen on 4 June that year, and complete performances followed in Bergen on 19 January 1865 and 28 November 1867. In the same year on 23 March Grieg conducted the last three movements at a Philharmonic Society concert in Christiania, but after 1867 he never allowed the Symphony to be performed again, although he published an arrangement of the middle movements for piano duet as *Two Symphonic Pieces*, Op. 14.

On his death the manuscript, clearly marked in Grieg's hand 'never to be performed', passed to the Bergen Public Library, who honoured the composer's injunction by never allowing it to leave the reading room. About seventy-three years later, a Soviet musicologist, taking advantage of the recently installed self-service xerox and the very relaxed atmosphere of the friendly staff, clandestinely made a copy to take back to Russia to perform. The Library authorities then felt that it would be best to arrange an official performance, and this was duly given at the Bergen Festival in the spring of 1981. The Bergen Symphony Orchestra was conducted by their resident conductor Karsten Andersen, and a commercial recording by the same artists was issued simultaneously. A further performance on disc by Okku Kamu and the Gothenburg Symphony Orchestra appeared in 1982. The full score was first published in volume eleven of the Grieg Complete Edition, which was printed in 1984, and a miniature score was issued by Peters. Thus, after its sleep of over a hundred years, the Symphony in C minor can be, and is, widely heard.

How is it to be assessed? First and foremost it is a very enlightening historical document, because it shows that although Grieg in later years constantly denigrated the education he had had at the Leipzig Conservatoire, at twenty years old he was fully capable of handling the full-length German symphonic form, and able to orchestrate in an adequate and workmanlike manner. Why it pleased Gade is easy to see. By this time he had turned his back on Scandinavian influences, regarding them as 'limiting' and 'unpromising', and his music cultivated the graceful melodies and unclouded harmonies of Mendelssohn's style. Here was a symphony which, although perhaps owing more to Schumann than Mendelssohn, yet cultivated the German idiom in the way of Gade's later symphonies. There was little in it of the Norwegian strangeness that Gade found so disturbing, and not at all to his taste, in Grieg's *Humoreskes* or Second Violin Sonata.

It was precisely for the reasons that Gade would have liked the work that Grieg decided to shelve it after 1867. A further reason was that Johan Svendsen's brilliantly novel and lively Symphony No. 1 also appeared this year, and Grieg understandably felt this was a far finer symphony than his own with which to blaze the trail into the Norwegian future. He therefore withdrew the symphony. Nevertheless the very occasional pointers to the mature Grieg in the work (for example, in the harmony and orchestration) make it interesting listening. One such pointer is the fecundity of *melodic* ideas. Although these are not yet the 'great' ideas which were to come, Grieg was clearly already finding it difficult to fit such a profusion into the balanced form of the German symphony.

Grieg's Symphony lasts rather more than half an hour and is scored for two flutes, two oboes, two clarinets, two bassoons, two horns, two trumpets, three trombones, percussion and strings – the same orchestra as Schumann's Second Symphony. The trombones are held in reserve for the last two movements, as in Schumann's Third Symphony, while his influence is also seen in the generally rather thick orchestration. It starts off in vigorous, bracing mood with a flourish of a few bars in which the trumpets are prominent, and then the first subject enters (Ex. 23):

Ex.23

The second subject, repeat of the exposition, development, recapitulation and coda all follow, entirely in keeping with the German mould. Pointers to later facets of Grieg's style include the harmonic spice given by false relations, and the picturesque scoring of some of the melodies for solo woodwind instruments. Then comes an *adagio* of exquisite melodic charm, and an *allegro energico* third movement in which the composer shows off some of the contrapuntal skill he had learned at the Conservatoire. The bracing mood of the first movement returns in the C major finale, which brings the Symphony to an exhilarating close.

Grieg's next orchestral work, the Overture *In Autumn*, Op. 11, gives a wonderful panorama of all the joy and picturesqueness of a Norwegian autumn. On a typical day in late September one can see farmers in the sunlit valleys gathering in the harvest, yet in the high hills the woodlands are already coloured yellow and golden brown, and up in the mountains the weather is cloudy and stormy, with bleak views and snow on the ground.

In appreciating Grieg's Overture, it is important to know that the Norwegian autumn embraces simultaneously all these varying aspects of the season: this saves English listeners from feeling that the widely contrasting moods depicted in quick succession are incongruous. In the introduction we are up in the hills, a cold wind is blowing, and although the gorgeous colours of the woodland are about us, life is ebbing from the countryside. The atmosphere becomes distinctly stormy with the first subject of the *allegro agitato*, a theme borrowed from Grieg's song *The Autumn Storm*, composed in 1865. One sometimes reads that the whole Overture is based on the song, but this is very misleading. The song, long and through-composed, deals not only with autumn storms, but aspects of the following winter and spring. Grieg only borrowed for his Overture the song's opening section, describing storm-gales stripping the foliage from the beech trees, and carpeting the ground with dead leaves. He specifically denied, in answer to a correspondent, that there were any thoughts of spring in his Overture.

The Overture, moreover, is much more wide-ranging in depicting autumn ideas, for the stormy first subject now gives way, via a melodious, wistful transition, to the second group of themes full of the season's warmth and fulfilment. The great abundance of melodies would have been ample to make up a suite of autumn miniatures, but Grieg, following the academic and critical expectations of the time, chose to cast them in the sonata-form of an overture. That meant that the exposition of all these wonderfully coloured themes now had to be followed by the development section. The effective contrasting of motifs from the introduction and the first subject, plus the working of the latter through a great many keys, show that Grieg had learned a great deal about development at the Leipzig Conservatoire. However, the glory of the Overture does not lie in these processes, rather in the moods and melodies, and these are only partially enhanced by the development.

Another matter altogether is the extended coda, based on a Norwegian traditional air which Grieg, in a footnote to the score, identifies as a Norwegian Reapers' Song. Here all the thrill and happiness of harvest time in the countryside are gathered up to form a triumphant paean. Scholars have argued about whether the folk-melody used is, or is not, a harvest song. But Grieg, as his note in the score shows, certainly accepted it as such, and wanted his audiences to as well. Also, scholars must not be too dogmatic here because the melody Grieg uses differs in some respects from any published source, and it may have been collected by Grieg or his brother. It certainly gives the composer's desired feeling of joyous life in the deep countryside, and is remarkable in the Overture as a unifying force (far more than the sonata-form) because the second theme of the second subject, as it appears in both exposition and recapitulation, is based on a rhythmic and melodic transformation of the 'Reapers' Song', which at the end stands revealed in its original form – a fitting climax.

The Overture was completed in 1866 and refused for publication by the Norwegian firm of Warmuth. The composer recalled that Gade, when shown the score, said, 'This is trash, Grieg; go home and write something better,' and Grieg did admit at the time that the work was poorly instrumented. He next arranged it for piano duet, and in this form it won a prize offered by the Swedish Academy, and was published in 1867. In 1887 Grieg re-scored the work. He himself conducted the first orchestral performance at the Birmingham Festival of 1888, for which the programme note, presumably authorised by Grieg, again described the final melody of the Overture as a harvesters' song.

We saw above how Grieg, on hearing of his friend Nordraak's death, immediately wrote a Funeral March for piano. Settled in Christiania, late in 1866, rightly realising how effective it would be for band, Grieg orchestrated his March for brass instruments and percussion. In this form it was performed at one of his subscription concerts on 12 December 1867. The autograph score of this version is in the Bergen Public Library, as is that of a later, fuller orchestration by Grieg for military band. This latter version was published by Peters in 1899. The instrumentation is for flauto piccolo in E flat, flauto di terza, two clarinets in E flat, two clarinets in B flat, two oboes, two cornets in B flat, two trumpets in E flat, two horns in E flat, two bassoons, alto trombone, two tenor trombones, two tubas, side drums, bass drum, cymbals and tamtam. The band versions are transposed up a semitone to B flat, to be more suitable for the wind instruments, but otherwise all closely follow the piano original. Other hands have tried their skill at scoring this March: for Grieg's funeral Johan Halvorsen prepared a version for full symphony orchestra; while a brilliantly effective arrangement for brass and percussion has been made recently by Philip Jones, who has broadcast and recorded it with his own Brass Ensemble.

For Edvard and Nina Grieg's summer holiday in 1868, a two-room cottage with a piano was booked for them at Søllerød near Copenhagen by two young friends, who lived nearby – the Danish composer Emil Horneman, and the Norwegian pianist Edmund Neupert (who had just been appointed professor of the piano at the Copenhagen Conservatoire). The Griegs arrived in Denmark in early June, left their two-month-old baby daughter with Nina's parents, and set off for the cottage. Grieg was burning with an intense desire to write a large-scale work, which his teaching duties and concert-giving in Christiania during the last two years had made quite impossible. It was arranged that the four friends, all in their mid-20s, would only meet in the evenings, at the inn in the small town; and often Neupert would take Nina out for the day to leave Grieg the solitude he found necessary for composing. In this idyllic summer, far away from any cares or problems, Grieg wrote his largest work – the Piano Concerto in A minor, Op. 16.

The key to this remarkably successful work is to understand that it is open-air music. It can only be appreciated fully by one who knows the music of wind, rain, clouds, lakes and sunsets. Thus the fine, manly emotions of the Concerto are continually moderated by the world of nature, which prevents them being too intense, or too unhealthily introspective. The many moods of the first movement are all felt against a landscape between hills and sea, now stormy, now sunny. The contentment and fulfilment of the slow movement is lit by the slow-moving colours of the Scandinavian summer sunset. The last movement is above all music of June; its happiness and hope seen against the clarity of midsummer light and the bright freshness of the countryside.

For once, too, Grieg does not seem to be having any problems with form. This is partly because he models this aspect of his Concerto on Schumann's A minor Concerto. The parallel features in the construction of the two first movements are particularly noticeable: the downward flourish for the piano at the start; the first subject in two contrasted sections announced by the orchestra and then played again by the piano; the fully written-out cadenza after the reprise; and the coda in faster tempo. Yet if Schumann's work gave Grieg an admirable *pattern* to follow, he filled it with his own original ideas. Schumann in 1841 was interested in mono-thematicism, and his second subject and first movement coda are developed from his main theme. Grieg, on the other hand, creates two new themes for his second subject, and yet another for his coda; and the extraordinary wealth of melodic gifts that the Concerto evinces is one of its main attractions.

The opening of the Concerto, with its crescendo drum-roll, loud chord for the whole orchestra, and descending figure for the piano, at once arrests attention. The descending run is built on the Grieg Motif and, as this Motif appears also in many other places in the Concerto, it gives a certain unity to the structure.

The first subject contains two main ideas: the initial one somewhat wistful, especially if Grieg's off-the-beat accents in the first and third bars are observed (which is not always the case in performances) (Ex. 24(a)); and the second more flowing and windswept (b):

Ex.24

An *animato* transition leads to the second subject, whose contemplative opening (Ex. 25(a)) is discussed by the piano before it introduces a new *più animato* theme (b):

Ex.25
(a)

mf *cantabile più tranquillo* —————— f —————

Meno tranquillo
(b) *cantabile*

The development section opens with a *tutti* based on the Grieg Motif, recalling the opening of the Concerto. This is followed by a bold continuation for cellos and basses. The rest of the development is mostly concerned with discussing the first subject, with attractive melodic fragments for solo flute and solo horn, accompanied by the soloist's swirling arpeggios. The recapitulation follows a regular course, and Grieg solves the cadenza problem not by leaving it out as Mendelssohn and Brahms did in their piano concertos but, like Schumann, in writing one himself. Grieg's solo part is extremely 'pianistic', one reason why so many concert pianists have the Concerto in their repertoire; but here, in the cadenza, the 'pianism' reaches its fullest, grandest expression: rapt contemplation alternating with hemi-demi-semiquaver bravura. Finally a quickening coda, in which the Grieg Motif intermingles with an enlarged version of the piano's opening flourish, brings the movement to a close.

The twenty-four bars of the hauntingly lovely theme that opens the *adagio* make an unusually long melodic statement for Grieg, and owe much of their charm to the two interrupted cadences that surprise the listener, and make him yearn for more (Ex. 26).

Ex.26

In the middle section the piano's ruminating arabesques lead gradually to an enriched statement of Grieg's opening theme accompanied by the orchestra. After a short link, bringing the listener back from D flat major to A minor, the piano announces the first subject of the finale (Ex. 27):

Ex.27

This has considerable expansion and discussion by soloist and orchestra, until the music modulates to F major for the second subject whose calm reflective theme (played by a solo flute), and slower tempo, make a striking contrast to what has gone before (Ex. 28):

Ex.28

The delicate orchestration continues when the piano softly takes up a restatement of this theme, for twenty bars accompanied only by a solo cello. The second subject too is now treated to some extension. Because his themes have been expanded in the exposition, Grieg is able to dispense with a development section, and moves on to the recapitulation. But the unexpected is still in store for the listener: the first subject makes a final appearance, transformed into 3/4 rhythm (Ex. 29):

Ex.29

and the second subject in its final statement, which brings the Concerto to its end, has a flattened seventh (Ex. 30):

Ex.30

Andante maestoso ♩ = 80

fff *pesante*

This was a most surprising harmonic and melodic inflexion for listeners at the time, as we see from the effect it made on Liszt. Grieg wrote to his parents from Rome on 9 April 1870, saying how he had been invited to go to Liszt's with a score of the Concerto, and how Liszt had sat down at the piano, and played it through at sight. When Liszt reached this point, the letter relates:

> He suddenly stopped, rose to his full height, left the piano and paced with stalwart, theatrical step and arm uplifted through the great hall of the monastery, while he fairly bellowed the theme. At the G natural, he stretched out his arm commandingly like an emperor and shouted, 'G, G, not G sharp'.

Then Liszt, after describing it as like an intoxicating liqueur, returned to the piano to play it again, and continued on to the end.

Edmund Neupert earned the dedication of the Concerto, which he had been accorded, by successfully giving the first performance of the work in Copenhagen on 3 April 1869, where it was well received, and following this up with performances in Christiania and Stockholm.

Critical opinion was, from the first, divided as to the merits of the Concerto. Germany's leading musical periodical carried hostile and cold reviews after the first German performance at Leipzig in 1872. On the other hand, the Concerto was much more favourably received at its English première at the Crystal Palace on 18 April 1874, when the soloist was Edward Dannreuther (formerly a fellow-student of Grieg's at the Leipzig Conservatoire). Though critical opinion was again divided, we find the *Monthly Musical Record* of May 1875 recalling the favourable impression the Concerto had made 'and the opinion very generally expressed at the same time that no more original or effective work of the kind had appeared since Schumann's Concerto in the same key'. The journal went on: 'We happen to know that many of our resident pianists, taking example from Mr Dannreuther, have set to work to study it. That it will eventually take its place as a stock piece among the best pianoforte concertos there can be little doubt.' At a time when many romantic concertos were appearing on the concert platform each year, this English critic showed remarkable perspicacity. But it accords with the generally very friendly notices in English periodicals of the 1870s that welcomed Grieg's compositions.

Grieg found it extremely difficult to get a publisher for the Concerto. A number of Danish and German firms refused it, believing it would never be viable. Finally in 1872 Svendsen was able to persuade his publisher Fritsch to bring out the work (although they had been amongst those that had earlier rejected it, sending it back to the composer with a note saying the piece was 'not interesting enough').

But the Concerto had not yet reached its definitive form, and when Fritsch brought out a second edition, ten years later, a number of changes had been made in the orchestration. In later years Grieg conducted performances with seventeen different pianists, who included Busoni, and in England Sir Charles Hallé, and he continued to mark his score with changes in instrumentation, new accents, marks of expression, and other small details. On 21 July 1907, only six weeks before his death, he listed all these, as well as adding parts for third and fourth horns, and sent them to Peters. These emendations were all incorporated in Peters' new edition of 1917.

But the story does not end even here, because the twenty-four-year-old Percy Grainger had arrived at Troldhaugen in the summer of 1907 to study the Concerto with Grieg before their performance planned for Leeds in September 1907. 'He is,' wrote Grieg, 'one of the most brilliant players I have ever heard; an artist and a man with astonishing depth and manysided talent,' and he went on to say that at the forthcoming Leeds Festival he thought Grainger would play the Concerto better than anyone. However, Grieg was taken ill just before leaving for England and died in hospital the following day. In 1919 Grainger published his edition of the Concerto with Peters, listing a number of further revisions, which he said had been authorised by Grieg.

The score of 1917, embodying the final revisions, for which Grieg took responsibility, is the edition invariably used today. There is no need to resurrect earlier versions, because virtually all the changes Grieg made were clarifications of what he wanted or improvements in the orchestration, which his increasing experience had enabled him to make.

WORKS FOR STRING ORCHESTRA

In the last quarter of the nineteenth century Romantic composers began again to cultivate the string orchestra, a medium which had largely lain dormant since the first half of the eighteenth century. Notable large-scale works included Dvořák's *Serenade* (1875), Tchaikovsky's *Serenade* (1881), and Elgar's *Serenade* (1893). Grieg showed a natural talent in scoring effectively for strings and added attractive works to the Romantic repertoire.

First came the *Two Elegiac Melodies*, Op. 34, of 1881. These are both based on songs (respectively Op. 33, no. 3, and Op. 33, no. 2) composed the previous year. In No. 1, *The Wounded Heart*, the poet says that after the sorrows and defeats of life he has retreated from the world; he suffers again each spring when the foliage opens and the cuckoo calls in the distance; but as the spring brings renewal to the earth, so also it brings solace to him. No. 2 initially bore the title *Spring*, the same as the song, but in later editions Grieg had this changed to *The Last Spring*, to warn conductors who did not know the original poem that this was not a song of rejoicing. In the text the poet marvels at the miracle of spring as the snow melts, the mountain rivers start flowing, the meadow turns green, and the lark sings. But, amidst all this beauty, he is heavy-hearted, feeling he is dying, and so it will be the last time he sees the wonders of springtide. The song ends with a mixture of gratitude for life and sadness at its ebbing.

Both songs are strophic, and Grieg presents the three verses of the former, and two of the latter song's original four verses, with widely differing instrumentation. Particularly lovely is the opening of verse two of *The Last Spring*, where the harmonies are carried high up by the violins divided into four parts and, throughout, the *divisi* writing brings rich and sonorous effects.

The *Holberg Suite*, Op. 40, has been discussed in the piano music section above, where the openings in both the piano original and the string orchestra version were compared. Felicitous string scoring continues on every page and, in its orchestral form, the work makes its best effect when played by large forces so that the solo lines for violin, viola and cello can be well contrasted, and the *divisi a 2* and *divisi a 3* sections sonorously executed. The five-movement suite shows Grieg at his best, and the new colourings the strings give to the grace and charm of the original make it a magnificent addition to the none-too-extensive string-orchestra repertoire.

In the *Two Melodies* for strings, Op. 53, Grieg once again chose two of his songs for transcription. No. 1, *Norwegian*, is based on the Vinje poem (Op. 33, book II, no. 6) about the value of the country dialect, Landsmål, as an artistic medium. The poet sees it as a good companion to the nationalist writer, striding into the future; and Grieg partners this idea with a resolute march. No. 2, *The First Meeting*, is based on the first of the *Four Songs from Bjørnson's Fisher Lass*, Op. 21: the poet compares the bliss of love at first sight to songs upon the water in purple evening shadows, and to distant horns sounding across scented heather, while music rises from two hearts that beat in sympathy. The string version captures, even more fully than the song, the rapture and ecstasy of first love – with the slow moving string-harmonies accompanying the ultra-expressive melody in the violins. The second verse is treated similarly to that in *The Last Spring*, with melody and harmonies carried high up by the violins alone, divided into four parts.

The final pair of string compositions is entitled *Two Nordic Melodies*, Op. 63. The first of these, *In Folk Style*, is a meditation on a dark, northern theme by an amateur musician, Fredrik Due, which fascinated Grieg. It is stated first in unison and then presented four times, on each occasion differently harmonised and scored, making the theme the basis for wonderful and often eerie effects. The eight minutes of the piece evoke a bleak and deserted northern landscape of bare mountains and icy lakes. No. 2, *Cowkeeper's Tune and Country Dance*, is based on two traditional melodies, already harmonised for piano by Grieg (Op. 17, nos. 2 and 18). These, one serene and the other cheerful, provide an admirable contrast to the first number. In the *Nordic Melodies* the string scoring once again abounds with subtle effects: as in no. 1, when one quarter of the cellos are directed to double below the 1st violins' octave melody (bars 93–97), or when various combinations of *arco* and *pizzicato* are used at the same time (e.g. no. 2, bars 57–62, and 67–72) or when sudden *decrescendos* are specified for chords from *fff* to *ppp* within a bar.

LATER ORCHESTRAL WORKS

Grieg, as already mentioned, re-orchestrated most of the *Peer Gynt* incidental music for a new production of the play in Copenhagen in 1886, and, hearing of its success, Dr Abraham wrote to enquire about its publication. Grieg, who, like Ibsen, never expected the play to be performed outside Scandinavia, wrote back that the problem was to produce an edition for concert use, and he would give thought to the matter.

In 1888 he re-orchestrated four of the pieces to form the *Peer Gynt*

Suite No. 1 (*Morning Mood – The Death of Åse – Anitra's Dance – In the Hall of the Mountain King* – their place in the drama is discussed above). Although they are selected somewhat randomly (as far as the plot goes), and integration – in the sense of key relationships or motivic cross-references – is lacking, yet Grieg achieved here a large-scale orchestral work, which quickly carried his name round the concert halls of the world. Audiences were at once attracted by the picturesqueness of the movements, whose titles gave just enough programmatic information to make their subjects enticing. The suite fitted well into the concert programmes of the day, as well as providing a refreshing contrast to the usual fare of overture – concerto – symphony. Also, Grieg had by now evolved a style of orchestration that admirably suited his music: for instance, the clearly sung woodwind melodies in *Morning Mood*, the idiomatic and carefully shaded string writing for *The Death of Åse* and *Anitra's Dance*, and the virtuosic and brilliant building of climax upon climax for *In the Hall of the Mountain King*.

There followed in 1891 the *Peer Gynt Suite* No. 2 (*The Abduction of the Bride and Ingrid's Lament – Arabian Dance – Peer Gynt's Homecoming – Solveig's Song*), once again most effectively re-orchestrated, with the song now delicately transcribed for flutes, clarinets, horns, harp and strings.

The success of these two suites, and his ever-present wish to write large-scale works, doubtless encouraged Grieg also to make a concert-suite from his music for *Sigurd Jorsalfar* in 1892. (The story of Bjørnson's play, and the context of the music in it, are also discussed above in the chapter on stage music.) For the *Prelude: In the King's Hall* he re-orchestrated *The Matching Game* from Act II; the second movement, *Intermezzo*, was *Borghild's Dream* in Act I; and the suite was completed with the *Homage March*, now inflated (and not entirely successfully) to over three times its original length. This is achieved by the addition of an opening and closing fanfare, the composition of a new middle section, and by the complete repetition, after it, of the whole first section. The March thus assumes ternary form, instead of the theatre-version's ever more majestic, natural growth.

The *Symphonic Dances*, Op. 64, published in 1898, are among Grieg's longest orchestral works, lasting a good twenty-five minutes. As the composer was known to have been working simultaneously on both the orchestral and the piano duet versions, there was some doubt about which was the original, but the composer made the matter clear in a letter of 10 April 1897 to Beyer, in which he said the *Symphonic Dances* were planned first of all as an orchestral work. However, as he was about to visit Denmark with Nina and wanted a new work to play, he wrote them down first as a piano duet, and then returned to working on the full orchestral score. The original conception of the *Symphonic Dances* as an orchestral work is confirmed by the autograph of the piano duet version, preserved in the Royal Academy of Music, Stockholm, which is headed: *Norwegian Dances for Orchestra* by Edvard Grieg, Op. 64, edition for piano, four hands. This manuscript also confirms the earlier completion of the piano duet version, being dated 'Troldhaugen, 27 September 1896', while Grieg's correspondence shows that he continued to be busy working on the orchestral version during 1897. The first performance of the latter was conducted by Johan Svendsen in Copenhagen on 4 February 1899, with the orchestra of the Royal Theatre.

The four movements are all based on dances collected by Lindeman for his *Old and New Mountain Melodies* – Grieg's major source for traditional material until the 1890s. Each dance is in strict ternary form; nevertheless, as with all Grieg's later music, the scoring is extremely effective. Particularly notable are the many melodies given to solo woodwind instruments, accompanied so unobtrusively that the solos sing out with the full expressiveness and beauty of their natural colour. The first dance uses a high-spirited *Halling* melody (Ex. 31 (a)), which is then melodically transformed by Grieg to make a pensive middle section (b):

Ex.31

(a) **Allegro moderato e marcato** ♩ = 112

(b) **Più lento** ♩ = 92

A coda, at first reflective, but then *presto*, brings the dance to an exhilarating close, with the trumpets playing an augmented version of Ex. 31 (a), bar one. The second dance has a truly enchanting melody, illustrating the origins in Norwegian folk-music of Grieg's favourite idea of varying a melody's opening phrase again and again. It is sung by the oboe accompanied by harp: both came over very clearly because the additional scoring consists only of divided violas and divided cellos (both low down in their range) and *pizzicato* basses (plus a few soft strokes on the triangle to add to the bucolic charm). The lightly scored middle section, in the contrasting tonic minor, provides delightful, colouristic solos for piccolo, flute, oboe, clarinet and bassoon, and its thematic material is based almost entirely on the Grieg Motif.

The third dance opens with two bold statements of the Grieg Motif, and then Grieg introduces a lively *Springing Dance*. As in the first dance, this is melodically transformed to make an *espressivo* middle section in the tonic minor. For the fourth dance Grieg uses an A minor traditional tune, *Did you see my love?* and a *Wedding Song* in A major, both of which he had harmonised earlier in his Op. 17 (nos. 23 and 24 respectively). But in this dance he seems determined to work on the largest possible canvas, with the A minor melody's eighteen bars of common time now the basis for the 260 bars of 2/4 which comprise the first section. Possibly the simple melody is stretched too far with its variants, extensions and augmentations. The *andante* and *allegro risoluto* introductions, as well as a number of short orchestral interludes, serve to increase the dark colouring. The cheerful *Wedding Song*, which then follows in the middle section, provides a pleasing and charming contrast. In this dance, above all, it would have been appropriate for the composer to provide a variant from the strict ternary form. But no, the whole long, first section is repeated with no alterations in the treatment or scoring, and a brief *presto* coda makes the ending. Notable among the interpreters of the *Symphonic Dances* was Sir Thomas Beecham, who extracted the ultimate liveliness from the sprightly dance rhythms, and was most graceful in accompanying the talented woodwind soloists he picked for his orchestras.

The tremendous popularity of Grieg in his last twenty years, and the demand for more works for concert hall use, next prompted him to orchestrate the *Old Norwegian Romance with Variations*, Op. 51, originally written for two pianos. It is very effectively done, and the composer deploys his large instrumental forces to colour the beautiful old romance and its various treatments to the full, which mitigate somewhat the monotony of the piano variations noted above.

After the first performance of the work in Christiania in 1904, conducted by Johan Halvorsen, and a further one in Copenhagen in 1905, conducted by Johan Svendsen, Grieg took their advice in making two extensive cuts: the second *andante* variation is deleted entirely; and then, eight bars before the end, thirty-two bars of the piano original are exchanged for four bars of orchestral 6/8. With these excisions, the orchestral *Variations* were published by Peters in 1906.

LYRIC SUITE (I SHEPHERD BOY; II GANGAR; III NOTTURNO; IV TROLLS' MARCH)

The German conductor Anton Seidl (1850–98), who had been Wagner's assistant at Bayreuth from 1872, orchestrated in 1895 four of Grieg's Lyric Pieces from Book Five (*Gangar, Bell-Ringing, Notturno, Trolls' March*) for use at the concerts he was directing with the New York Philharmonic Orchestra. In 1903 Grieg was sent the score, but did not feel able to agree to its publication because of the very heavy instrumentation. Many commentators have their doubts about how much of the version eventually published in 1906 is Seidl's and how much Grieg's, but the Bergen Public Library has a complete copy of Seidl's score written out neatly in ink by Grieg, and a comparison of the two scores answers the question exactly.

Firstly, Grieg made his own poetic orchestration for harp and strings of *Shepherd Boy* (a piece that did not appear in Seidl's score). Seidl had scored *Gangar* in its original key of C major, but Grieg's version is completely rethought and transposed up a tone to D major to increase the brightness of effect. In the *Notturno*, Grieg greatly simplifies an elaborate harp part of Seidl's and in the *Più Mosso* section replaces Seidl's long passages of fussy string semiquavers with simple string chords, against which the woodwind solos are much clearer. In the *Trolls' March*, although Grieg's score is clearly based on Seidl's, almost every page has small, telling alterations, which greatly enhance the music's colour and effectiveness, such as the addition of double basses to the opening ten bars, and the strengthening of melodic entries which are in danger of being submerged in Seidl's heavy brass accompaniments.

Seidl's orchestrations, with their thick doublings and heavy use of the brass, are reminiscent of late Wagner, and altogether unsuitable for these charming, water-colour miniatures of the Norwegian countryside. In the published *Lyric Suite*, only the third and fourth movements have any connection with Seidl, and as Grieg's orchestrations were carefully rethought to make the music more poetic, there seems no reason why biographers and encyclopaedists should still hesitate to add the *Lyric Suite* to their lists of Grieg's works. Grieg himself conducted the first performance in Christiania on 6 December 1905, and a further one with the Concertgebouw Orchestra in Amsterdam in April 1906. When the score was sent to Peters for printing, Grieg generously stipulated that any fee due to him for the orchestration was to be paid to Seidl's widow, and in due course she received a cheque for 1000 marks.

Grieg decided to withhold *Bell-Ringing* from inclusion in the *Lyric Suite*, feeling it was essentially piano music, and of a most idiomatic kind. His copy in the Bergen Library of Seidl's version has extensive changes made in ink, and hundreds of notes scratched out with a pen-knife, so it is impossible to see much of what Seidl wrote. The piece was used as a novelty to open the 1953 Bergen Festival, and continued to be used for succeeding Bergen Festivals, becoming something of a signature tune for these occasions. The full score was first published in 1983, in Volume 13 of the Grieg Complete Edition.

Conclusion

'The North is most assuredly entitled to a language of its own,' wrote Robert Schumann. Entirely apt! – as are most of his epigrams in literature and music. And just as a musical language for Spain has been provided by Albéniz and Falla, and for Russia by the 'Mighty Handful', so the dark colours, the solitude of nature, the bracing winds, the heritage of legends in the sagas and the *Kalevala* – and much else that epitomises the North – are represented for most music-lovers by the music of Grieg and Sibelius.

It is interesting to note how often the two composers chose the same subjects for their compositions, and to compare how each treated them, with Grieg usually working as a miniaturist and Sibelius composing on a broad symphonic canvas. Note, for instance, their reaction to the northern forests: in Grieg there is the tiny prelude to Act III of *Peer Gynt* of twenty-five bars for strings and horns, headed *In the Depths of the Pine Forest*; while in Sibelius there is the vast symphonic poem *Tapiola*. Each is a masterpiece; one like a small pencil drawing, the other a huge painting in oils.

Both composers conjured up an orchestral storm at sea: Grieg in *Peer Gynt*, Sibelius in the *Tempest* prelude. They were fascinated by man's relationship to nature and the poetry of the seasons – a theme that constantly recurs in their songs. Each depicted the northerner's joy in homecoming: Grieg in the Lyric Piece *Homeward*, Sibelius in *The Return of Lemminkainen*. Both portrayed a night ride: Sibelius's develops into a sunrise as the rider turns eastwards out of a dark forest; while Grieg's piano piece (from *Moods*, Op. 73) has a 'moonlit rendezvous' middle section. Grieg's Third Violin Sonata of 1886 and Sibelius's Violin Concerto of 1903 seem to inhabit very much the same emotional world. Both composers published one String Quartet, full of autobiographical self-communing; and the ending of Grieg's Piano Sonata, where the second subject moves ever more triumphantly forward, immediately brings to mind Sibelius's conclusion to his Third Symphony.

Other nationalist composers of the late nineteenth century, in seeking to break away from German domination, often had useful roots in the past music of their lands. Thus Mussorgsky was able to build on the foundations of Russian Orthodox liturgical music, and Debussy had the rich flowering of French music of the seventeenth and eighteenth centuries to turn to. Mussorgsky and Debussy also had able and successful nationalist composer-colleagues in their own countries as a stimulus.

Grieg, in pioneering Norwegian music, had no such advantage. His most distinguished Norwegian contemporaries, Svendsen and Sinding, made their reputation largely through writing music in the international style of the day. In the previous generation of Norwegian composers, Kjerulf introduced some national strains into his songs and piano music, while Ole Bull depicted national scenes though with a weak technique. But these composers, completely unrecognised internationally, were only of scanty help to Grieg. Building on such slight foundations and in such a lonely environment, it is an outstanding achievement that he was still able to forge such an original, splendid Norwegian style, and secure wide and continuing recognition. His style, moreover, was to be an important influence on composers of the next generation such as Delius, Ravel and Percy Grainger, while providing an enduring inspiration to many Norwegian composers of today, who continue to pay him tribute.

The Name Of Grieg

Girig, King of Scotland 878–889, was the source of the modern Scots surname Greig, which is found especially in Fife and along the central east coast. In medieval Scottish documents Girig's successors are found having their names spelt variously as Greg, Grige and Grege. In sixteenth-century parish records the name appears as Gregg, Grieg and Grig. It is interesting then that the great-great-grandfather of the Norwegian composer, who lies buried in the churchyard of Rathen West, near Fraserburgh, has his name spelt first as John Grieg and then as John Greig in the obituary notice carved on his tombstone. The stone's engraving records that it was erected to his memory by his surviving children after his death on 6 January 1774. It is not likely that they would have allowed the stonemason to get it wrong, so John probably used both forms, Grieg and Greig.

John Greig's son Alexander (1739–1803) spelt his name Greig while he was in Scotland, but soon after settling in Bergen in 1779 changed the spelling to Grieg. In doing so he was probably only reverting to one of the forms used by his father. Alexander was the founder of the Norwegian branch of the family.

Grieg's Manuscripts

The manuscripts which the Bergen Public Library received under the terms of Grieg's will consisted of sketches, unfinished works, and a number of pieces composed up to 1882. After he had signed an exclusive contract with Peters in 1883, his manuscripts were usually sent to Leipzig, as soon as completed, and used as printer's copy. It was long thought that these had been lost during the ravages of the Second World War, when Leipzig was devastatingly bombed.

However, to avoid Nazi persecution, the youngest son of the Jewish family that owned Peters, Robert Hinrischen, had made his way to London in the 1930s, carrying with him 300 pages of Grieg's manuscripts, comprising 29 compositions. He kept the information to himself, and at his death in 1981 bequeathed them to his sister-in-law Mrs Evelyn Hinrischen in New York, who for a long time did not realise what she had under her care. Mrs Hinrischen wished them to return to Grieg's homeland and offered them in one lot to the Norwegian government, who sent over Professors Dag Schjelderup-Ebbe and Finn Benestad of Oslo University to authenticate them.

On 20 December 1985 it was announced that the Norwegian government had paid US $614,000 to acquire them (plus some 375 letters from the composer to his publishers), and that they are to be added to the Bergen Public Library's Grieg Archive. A full editorial commentary will appear in volume 20 of the Grieg Complete Edition.